DUE NORTH by
Lola Akinmade Åkerström

Books may be purchased by contacting the publisher
and author at:

Publisher: Geotraveler Media Sweden
Stockholm, Sweden
Phone: +46765589733
Email: lola@geotravelermedia.com
Web: www.geotravelermedia.com

Cover Design:
Lilit Kalachyan-Nurse, Lola Akinmade Åkerström

Interior Design:
Lilit Kalachyan-Nurse / lknbranded.com

Editor: Amanda Castleman

ISBN: 978-91-983913-0-5 (print)

ISBN: 978-91-983913-1-2 (eBook)

Printed in the United States

DUE NORTH

A Collection of Travel Observations, Reflections, and Snapshots Across Colors, Cultures, and Continents

We pass a "cow crossing" sign. To my left stand the sheer cliff faces of Italy's Madonie Mountains covered with thick brownish vegetation.

I look to my right.

Generously spaced barriers prevent cars from nosediving over the edge. I wonder where the cows are coming from.

Within seconds, my husband and I swerve sharply to the right as a Fiat Panda barrels down the middle of the narrow road, quickly disappearing around a bend. Eight kilometers (5 miles) into our harrowing ascent, I'm not so sure the 13-room spa resort is worth the nerve-racking trek. If anything, our equally terrifying ride back down was bound to negate any relaxation we'd planned.

"Keep right. Continue 4km (2.4 miles)," the GPS unit coos in an American accent. Thick magenta lines on its screen indicate our uphill route, but now the never-ending switchbacks look like a toddler's crayon scribbles. The black-and-white checkered flag signaling our destination seems to be playing digital chess with us.

The spa read like a dream on paper. It promised solace within the Sicilian countryside, far away from the chock-full-o'-tourists seaside village of Cefalù along the Tyrrhenian Sea. And solace couldn't come soon enough as we'd taken in our daily fill of tanned potbellies spilling over tight flesh-cutting Speedos.

As we climb, the sun slowly dives behind the warm blue waters below, rewarding us with one of those sunsets one tries to describe but miserably fails at. To avoid a dive of our own, though, our eyes remain firmly locked on the snaking road ahead.

With each kilometer traveled, we lose inches of maneuvering space as it gets narrower.

"Recalculating, turn left," the GPS starts. Turning left means crushing our car like a soda can into the side of the mountain, so we slow down and poke nervously at the navigation unit. If we could shake it like a Magic 8 Ball to get a different answer, we would because the inevitable has happened. We are desperately lost.

"Let's switch it to British English," my husband suggests.

"British English?"

"Yes!"

"Why?"

"Why not?"

We switch it and get a different set of directions up the mountain. "Keep right. Continue 5km [3 miles]."

Following the Brit's accent seems to work as we see a sign for Gratteri, the village where our spa is located. Thick rain clouds loom overhead and we feel like hobbits on a quest in our little Peugeot. Adding the apt mystical setting we need, sun rays spill through heavy clouds resting over the Aeolian Islands far out at sea.

Relief comes momentarily as we see semblances of village life: rusty earth-tone structures carved right out of the countryside. We turn onto a stony path, our car just small enough to pass between buildings.

"Recalculating..." the Briton finally fails us.

"I'm switching it to Swedish," my husband yells, retreating to his mother tongue.

"Wait!" I point ahead to a small Fiat hatchback with "*polizia*" scribbled across it. We drive up to a single barricade and an officer instinctively walks up.

"*Buona sera* (good evening)," I greet him, half rolling down my window. "Belli?" I namedrop the spa.

"Ha!" he yells in recognition. He gives us perfect directions in Italian, hands gesturing and curving like snakes as he describes what we are bound to encounter en route and how we'll find it.

"*Grazie*," we thank him without understanding a single word and back away. Our last hope remains our now Swedish-speaking GPS. Like an 8 Ball, it gives us yet another set of directions.

"*Sväng höger* (turn right)."

Having made peace with the mountain gods at this point, we roll up what seems like the final stretch of road leading right to the summit. We pass through dark brooding clouds before turning down a cobblestone path. Three bespectacled, beshawled grandmothers stop mid-conversation and stare, as we screech to a stop. Two lines of middle-aged ladies are calmly filing through the intersection. They wear black with dark magenta details across their chests and all carry lit candles. Leading the procession is a young man heaving a large golden cross.

Church bells chime along with sheep bells in the distance and shoes gently tap as the procession climbs slowly and serenely up to the village church that Sunday evening in Gratteri. For the first time since our angst-riddled search began, calm washes over us.

The GPS feels it too. "*Ankommer målet* (arriving at destination)," it suddenly announces.

A couple feet from the church lay the spa.

TABLE OF CONTENTS

DUE NORTH 5

Table of Contents 9

Dedication 13

About the Cover Image 15

Foreword 17

Preface 18

My Little Green Book 11

SOUTH 20

Back to Sender 25

Our Engagement or Yours? 28

Walkway to Nowhere 33

Fijian Rose 36

The Reader in 26A 38

PHOTO SPOTLIGHT
Notes on Zainab & Finding Talent in Corners 42

WEST 48

High Street 53

From Manicures to Machu Picchu 56

I Pledge Allegiance 60

Sweet Pillows 64

Hanging with Cesenatico's Fishmongers 71

Waking up with Fishmongers 74

Notes on Marriage, Space, & Travel from Paco 79

The Sicilian Countryside 82

PHOTO SPOTLIGHT
The Terracotta Life 84

TABLE OF CONTENTS CONTINUED

EAST **93**

My Polish Informant 96

A Convergence at Sue's 98

Trafficking Innocence 103

Kwang Yaw 107

PHOTO SPOTLIGHT
Slow Traveling through Markets 110

NORTH **118**

Port of Call 123

Dear Annikki 126

One Fine Swedish Day 132

The Light Chasers 139

Decoding *Lagom* 144

PHOTO SPOTLIGHT
The Crayfish Experience 153

Final Thoughts **161**

Brown-Eyed Girl Meets Blue-Eyed Boy 162

About the Author 173

Special Thanks 173

DEDICATION

To the Urb... my compass guiding me north.

ABOUT THE COVER IMAGE

On a warm spring day, I was visiting the small community of Ccaccaccollo, deep within the Sacred Valley in Peru. I wanted to observe the women — skilled weavers — working the looms, weaving alpaca fibers, and mixing dyes in cauldrons.

As they worked, a young Quechua boy came skipping along a red mud wall and, for a split second, hung frozen in time like a historic painting — a symbol of absolute joy. That moment of pure innocence was forever ingrained in my mind. He instantly transported me back to my childhood, a time when I found total excitement in the most basic things.

As I turned back to the women at the looms, their work became much more vibrant and extraordinary.

The author as a teenager in boarding school in Nigeria.

FOREWORD

Notes on Joanna, Tété-Michel, and Visions Pointing North

"It feels as if [the Northern Lights] knew we wanted it so badly and instead of giving just a little bit of light or a bit of green — and I would have been so grateful for that — instead we got the whole business."

—Joanna Lumley

Joanna Lumley leaned towards Professor Truls Lynne Hansen, who'd been explaining how solar particles collide with the earth's gases to her. She was holding a book, an Australian children's book. Joanna quickly flipped to a specific page she had admired for decades and pointed to the penguin.

A penguin named Ponny. She was looking up at an illustrated curtain of light rippling across the dark sky.

"See," said Joanna, then 52 years old, sitting up a little taller as she showed off Ponny to the professor.

As an army child growing up in Malaysia, she'd read books filled with snow, trolls, and the Northern Lights. Something had frozen Ponny the Penguin in her tracks. Something that demanded her full attention, and as a child, Joanna vowed she would see what Ponny saw.

What had stopped Ponny so, as she gazed northwards?

As the years passed, she would find out that Ponny was actually looking at the Southern (not Northern) Lights, but that meant nothing. To her, Ponny was looking northwards.

I studied Joanna. I recognized something about her. Her demeanor. That uncontrollable excitement. I saw flashes of the child who'd spent years looking at Ponny. Who'd never experienced snow in Malaysia.

Finally making her way to Tromsø in northern Norway, she saw those curtains dance across the sky.

She broke down.

And then I broke down, because I understood.

During his 1950s teenage years, Tété-Michel Kpomassie found a children's book about Greenland at a local Jesuit library in Togo. He vowed he would see this landscape, so drastically different from his own.

For the next 12 years, he journeyed through West Africa and continental Europe, making his way north until finally catching a boat to Greenland.

I am currently reading Tété-Michel's journey. I know I will break down again.

In the 1990s, I had an encounter with a book too. A map. In a geography class in Nigeria.

My eyes followed lines. Latitudes. Longitudes. The Greenwich Meridian. The Tropics of Cancer and of Capricorn. My eyes went north. They rested on a point at the very top of the world.

"I will reach the North Pole," I said to my teenage self... And it remains my elusive goal.

PREFACE

My Little Green Book

I know what's coming. I'd gone through this drill dozens of times. As many times as each of those vibrant and colorful visas in my little green book, my Nigerian passport. Even before the immigration officer pulls me aside, I instinctively pull myself aside.

He glosses over my visa. A visa I've spent hundreds of dollars acquiring. He finds his government's issued permission, but curiosity gets the better of him. He thumbs through the rest, looking through the two green passports stapled together because the visas had outnumbered the pages.

"Why all these visas?" he asks.

This scene was repeated in airport after airport across several continents. The more visa stamps in my passport, the more my motives for travel were deeply questioned.

Why was I traveling?

There had to be a more sinister reason beyond the need to explore and enrich my life through experiencing other cultures. There had to be a dubious reason for me to leave my comfortable bubble of familiarity and travel the world to put my life in perspective as a global citizen. There had to be a mysterious reason why I would want to sample traditional foods, trace the steps of history, and marvel at architecture so grand that I stand awe-struck in silence.

Because that explanation — the deep enrichment travel brings into our lives — was too easy an explanation for every immigration officer reviewing my Nigerian passport.

I remember taking my first bus tour through Eastern Europe right before several countries joined the E.U. in 2004. In hindsight, I should have waited a year. But life itself isn't guaranteed, opportunities should be taken when presented, and waiting would have defeated the pull and wanderlust of travel.

So that meant paperwork for every single country — five of them — that I was traveling through on that trip: Poland, Slovakia, Hungary, Austria, and the Czech Republic. Close to $1,000 in multiple-entry visa fees alone.

At border crossings, our rowdy group of 20-somethings fell silent each time a passport control officer hopped on board and glided down the aisle, sucking away our collective air with authority. Grabbing various blue (U.S) and red (E.U.) passports and neatly stacking them, he'd stop by my seat. After a glance at my green passport as if it were a contraband item, he'd study my face and push my document beneath the pile.

At every single border, I'd convince myself it was for easier access, that mine was pushed beneath the pile. Until the officer would come back onto the bus and escort me off for further questioning with his colleagues.

Why was I traveling? Explaining it to one officer was never enough. I had to elaborate this unbelievable concept of a Nigerian traveling for the sole purpose of enjoyment to his colleagues too.

By the time our tour through Eastern Europe was over, I'd inadvertently delayed our bus for an average of 30 minutes at each border crossing, when I was the one who had paid almost a grand to have my motives scrutinized and travel sanctioned.

But the beautiful irony is that my little green book opened up the world to me.

While doors were being slammed, it stubbornly wedged itself through the cracks and got me in. It filled me with an undeniable resolve and passion to keep exploring and learning about the world around me. Above all, it kept me truly listening to people and their cultures, what they believe and why they live the way they do.

It forced strangers to see me, deal with me, and learn about me even when they weren't ready to. And in my own way, I began to chip away at their biases, distrust, and discomfort around people they didn't encounter every day.

Today, I work as a travel writer and blogger, sharing rich cultural stories of everyday folk, their lifestyles, their traditions, and what makes them burn with unbridled passion. I also communicate these stories visually as a photographer within the National Geographic brand. Ironically, I have an E.U. passport now: one that came because I found love across borders. And the ease with which I can flow through those very same boundaries and cultures is without a doubt a privilege. It's one I certainly don't take for granted.

Traveling with my Nigerian passport has never weakened my resolve, but I can't help wondering. How many talents lay hidden forever because people were never given the opportunity to explore, to see the world, to learn from other cultures, to be cultural ambassadors themselves, and to use those talents to make a difference in their own way?

How easy it could have been for me to become demoralized after the umpteenth border stop, after paying yet another $200 visa fee, after feeling the emotional weight of never-ending restrictions simply because I was born in a certain country!

I will never forget my little green book. It was what drove me to explore the world. To keep stubbornly pushing past boundaries and barriers in life. To realize this was the career path I was born to be on.

It was what taught me resilience and perseverance.

SOUTH

The Seychelles

Our family trip to the Seychelles remains one of our favorite memories together, from feeding Aldabra giant tortoises to learning to cook the best grouper curry with Chef Sherla Mitsi Mathurin.

I was six months pregnant and on assignment, which involved island-hopping with Jerry and Leopold, and getting a glimpse into their passionate world of octopus hunting and deep sea fishing.

I went out with them to pull up the traps. I'll never forget the joy on Jerry's face when he lifted the first one to find it full. I learned to love what I do from these Seychellois fishermen — even if it means starting at 6am on the gloomiest of days.

That trip serves as a constant reminder to keep weaving journeys into our lifestyle, because it's so easy to make travel a novelty. We need to keep cultivating that curiosity — whether far away or in our own backyard.

That curiosity is what makes us engaged explorers.

Back to Sender

Through loud speakers connected to a van, a heavily synthesized voice belts out "Back to sender, O! Back to sender!"

These are the only English lyrics in the Muslim worship song he sings in Yoruba, a West African language. The rusty, once-white van is parked along a one-way street, yet traffic travels in both directions — a common scene in my hometown of Lagos, Nigeria.

A poster of a deceased local engineer and mentor hangs next to a "good luck" sign, both pasted on a small bus designed for 12 passengers, but clearly holding about 40. Faces press against its windows, as the riders wait

24

patiently for the extra passenger the bus conductor is certain can fit in comfortably.

More buses roll past, emerging from a steamy lot across from the music-blasting van. Stickers of "Adam's Desire," a sexual enhancer, are fixed to the bumpers and rear windows of some. Others have biblical quotes and references to God's absolute might and protection. Patrons choose buses guided by how they feel spiritually on any particular day.

Okadas (motorcycle taxis) race up and down the street, buzzing and narrowly dodging cars, as well as vendors selling oranges, phone cards, snacks, and other random items. They sit close to the edge of the street with their toes within inches of rolling tires. The *okada* drivers sport helmets, not because they want to, but because of a newly instated law. Many helmets remain unbuckled or perched atop caps and *geles* (head ties worn by women).

There is a constant sense of mortality. Pedestrians and vendors dart through oncoming traffic with cat-like reflexes. All senses are heightened. The sweltering heat so violates the mind that one retaliates with aggression to stay alive.

Not quite ready to jump into the maddening flow, I temporarily slip into the Nigerian daze to survive. This semi-conscious state allows one to stare with no facial expression at everything; not fully observing and yet subconsciously aware of one's surroundings.

Hours can be spent waiting, sitting, wandering, and relaxing within this state. I'd hoped it would conserve my sanity... but I am jolted back when a tanker truck sideswipes my little sister's car violently. This intentional act leaves me perplexed.

"You need just the right amount of madness in this town," she announces. "Give them the illusion that you're ready to snap any second."

He'd cut us off and our frustrated driver had given him the "waka" sign — right palm open, fingers arched, and a quick flick at the elbow toward the recipient. This means "God punish your mother!"

The trucker had been ready to kill us for insulting him and had rammed into our car, shoving us off the road. Minutes earlier, a dilapidated tow truck had cut us off and thrown the "waka!" sign at the sound of our frustrated horn. Personal insult is feigned as a way of bullying to get ahead.

Just a few days ago, another tanker had run over a woman — who'd probably wandered into its path — crushing her until her entrails burst loose in full view of everyone.

In the midst of it all, air-conditioned sedans, borderline airtight, seem to glide through the frenzy. Uniformed school kids stare out windows, their noses pressed against chilled glass, observing the sweltering exterior world. Wondering what it sounded like, as people, cars, and buses all seemed to move by in slow motion to them.

Early afternoon meant they were probably headed to after-school lessons. I watch them with a sense of familiarity.

I could easily recount their days, hour by hour. They probably woke up this morning to either Christian or Muslim prayers, took a bath from a warm pail of water, scarfed down a breakfast of bread and tomato-onion omelets, and got carted off to school. They screamed the national anthem at the top of their lungs, as competitive juices began to bubble to the surface. Then the children would compete to be first to ask questions in class, arms shooting up like referee flags on offside calls.

The goal: to be seen and heard.

Life is lived day to day in Nigeria's largest city. Most meals are cooked and completely consumed the same day, as refrigerators are at the mercy of the erratic electric company and small generators. So open air farmers' markets thrive. Sole proprietorships thrive. Daily routine pulsates at feverish pitches. Nigerians are alive today and this fact is celebrated with noise, organized chaos, aggression, and a sharpened sense of the "now."

People exist vibrantly here and they need to. For any minute, they could very well be sent back to sender.

"You need just the right amount of madness in this town," my little sister hints at her mad-dog survival strategy, as she skillfully steers a large SUV through thick Lagos go-slow traffic on another occasion. "Give them the illusion that you're ready to snap any second."

One only spews from experience in this city and *okada* drivers remain the main traffic nuisance, whizzing by and squeezing between vehicles like mosquitoes, oblivious to merging buses and cars switching lanes.

"Madam, wetin dey do you?" one biker yells in pidgin

English after almost crashing head-on into my sister's SUV in an attempt to squeeze by as she makes a perfectly legal right turn.

She quickly rolls down her window and lets out a crazed laugh.

"You want to die? You want to die?" she yells back vehemently. "I go send you back to your maker!" She ends with a cackle.

The driver gives her the "waka" sign and speeds off.

As her maniacal laughter dies down, I turn to her. She'd been one of those little school kids wearing blue-and-white checkered gingham uniforms with large blue collars, taking in the world from the backseat, with her little nose pressed against a chilled glass window.

We'd both been.

Our Engagement or Yours?

Rain falls. Not hard, but just enough to give my sisters and I a few minutes to collect ourselves and observe the world through tinted windows. A few feet away, uninvited cameramen stand in the light drizzle, waiting for us — the bride and her siblings — to emerge. The photographers are a tradition at these ceremonies... taking pictures of people, which they develop within minutes and try to sell back to the unsuspecting subjects.

There is already a frenzy of activity... women in colorful traditional attires called "aso okes" mill around. Their geles (head ties) perch at impossible angles on their heads, defying gravity.

We watch as the caterers transfer meals from their vans to the hall. We can tell them apart from guests who decided to bring their own food and voluntarily contribute to the event. We see the traditional batá drummers run from arriving guest to exiting guest, playing and praising them in our language in the hopes of getting "sprayed"... a term for receiving money on your forehead, neck, or any other body part instead of in your hands.

This is the first engagement in my immediate family. We are excited to celebrate my sister Dami's joy.

Invitations had already been printed and sent out on her behalf, so most of the guests look unfamiliar. We can't hide our glee when we spot a familiar face... followed by unfamiliar face after unfamiliar face after semi-familiar face, all filing into the hall.

Already an hour late, my three other sisters and I decide to go in, leaving the bride behind. The ceremony will start whenever our parents want it to... regardless of what was printed on the invitations. We walk into a hall filled with colorful attire: greens for the groom's side and purples for the bride's. Even guests with no blood ties still come dressed in supporting hues. And everyone has already started eating and reveling in a sinful, yet luxurious, manner.

Three bands are playing simultaneously, each refusing to give the other a moment of spotlight. So we have traditional Calabar dancers moving among the guests, gyrating and shaking to gospel music belted out by another team. We stand rooted, trying to absorb all that is going on around us. When we are ready, we are expected to jump into the flow.

"Take one!" A random lady semi-yells at me, poking me with a gift item. I look at it. The plastic fan has a picture of my sister and her fiancé printed on it with "congratulations!" I study it. This has not been sanctioned by my family. The guests and extended family members are bringing presents to share with each other, just like the coolers of food and crates of drinks they'd contributed. Soon enough, we are handed plastic containers, handkerchiefs, scarves, and pens from different individuals, all with pictures or words celebrating the newly engaged couple.

My sisters and I stroll over to the table that holds the typical Nigerian gifts from the groom's relatives to our family. Tubers of yams, crates of beer, sacks of rice, bottles of wine, a hamper basket, boxes of biscuits... some of which we all guess correctly based on their wrapped shapes.

More and more items are brought in and added to the pile. At this moment, my siblings and I share a smile. The day's start had given us a taste of what was to come. Way before the crack of dawn, we'd started changing into traditional attire, navigating through a maze of 30 — yes, 30 — relatives who had decided to come spend the night, prepare us, and carpool to the festivities.

We are now an hour and a half late, and the traditional engagement ceremony hadn't officially started. An outsider looking in would think "total chaos," but in my culture this is one of the ways we express love and support. Our selfless need to tirelessly work and celebrate on one another's behalf is something I am proud of. We take the concept of sharing to a new level. For us Yoruba, "community" is not just another word.

We live and breathe it. It takes a community to raise children, teach children, acknowledge their successes, encourage them when they fail, and celebrate their engagements and weddings. A Nigerian engagement isn't really about you, so much as an opportunity for family, friends, and friends of friends to reunite and reminisce on your behalf. Everyone is your auntie, uncle or cousin.

So bringing more food and gifts to your ceremony is an obligation they joyfully bask in, not an inconvenience. "*Mo gbo, mo ya*" (I heard, I stopped by) means that if I discovered someone was getting engaged or married, I would swing by and celebrate. Official invitations exist just as a courtesy.

As I observe the genuine happiness and warmth that emanates from the people moving around, eating, dancing, and sharing, I smile. The engagement party could have been anyone's... but it was everyone's too.

Walkway
to Nowhere

"You this idiot man!" Seyi yells at Samson. Both men are generator vendors whose market stall I am in one hot summer day in Lagos, Nigeria.

"Why are you listening to Fashola?"

Samson is leaning in close to a parked car, listening to the governor's latest decree about *okadas* (motorcycle taxis) in Lagos, where I grew up. The radio blasts through the open window, but the driver himself remains fast asleep on a reclined car seat.

"When he talks, you better listen to him, O!" Samson retorts with a belly laugh. I sense his mild tang of sarcasm. The air is pregnant with African humidity. After two failed generators and a few days without electrical power, my family has come to Idumagbon market in search of solutions. That summer afternoon found me seeking shelter from the shocking heat underneath a soiled tarp that was protecting stacked generators.

My mother has been haggling for the last 20 minutes with one of their business partners. From his knife-in-the-stomach reaction to her initial offer, I know they'll be going at it for awhile. She introduces the fact that she'd bought another generator — the second to blow up in one week — from this very shop. Their haggling session is shifting rapidly from barter to reprimand.

I slip into the Nigerian daze to wait out their transaction; mentally checked out, yet subconsciously aware of the bustle around me.

"Why should I listen? Do Fashola and I have business together?" Seyi's anger seemed a little excessive.

"I guess someone doesn't like him," I joke.

"Can you imagine what he did?" Seyi prepares to unload. "He is building a walkway on that cross street over there for bankers and pedestrians!"

His reasoning escapes me. A walkway sounds pretty harmless, if not long overdue. "He chased the traders all away, pushing them away from the street!" They lost their sole source of sustenance, he points out.

I'd visited Lagos the year before, but this time around, the city seems different and cleaner. The stuffy mob scenes at the airport immigration desks had been replaced with queues guided by dividers. The street hawkers who once wove in and out of traffic, selling fried plantain chips and other snacks, seem few and far between. Women — wearing orange uniforms and sometimes, yellow vests over long African attire called *ankaras* — are sweeping the streets with wooden brooms, as motorcycles and buses whizz by within inches. Patches of land where makeshift markets once stood had been cleared.

"Thank God for Fashola!" people cry at almost every street corner. Something else is in the air besides the stench of garbage; a certain sense of hope that some order could be brought into one of the most chaotic cities in the world.

The governor's brushstroke of change can be seen all over — dabbed here and there to enhance the city's beauty, and his shovel is excavating improvised communities to bring in some zoning.

Seyi's rants seem borderline blasphemous.

"Ha! Mommy!" Our conversation is instantly broken when the businessman yells. Vendors usually refer to patrons older than themselves by "mommy" or "daddy." If patrons are about the same age, then it's "my sister" or "my brother."

My mother has cut into the negotiated price yet again.

I wonder why he keeps going. He'd already sold her a flawed generator once. Maybe he's trying to get rid of more, disguising their unreliability with dramatic flares of disbelief at the prices she suggests?

Samson leaves the car's side to join us. "Do you know what I have to do this evening?" he says. I know it's not a question. "I have to go help this *alhaji* sell his car to feed his family!"

I come to find out that the *alhaji* — a term used for Muslim men who've taken the *Hajj* pilgrimage to Mecca — is one of the squeezed-out street vendors. After his displacement, he hadn't been able to bounce back. Six months later, Samson is going to help him liquidate his asset.

The nearby haggling becomes a low, muffled, semi-heated exchange; the businessman defending his products, my mother refuting his recommendations, while she tries to purchase a new generator. The verbal tango of logic they dance remains our background entertainment.

"[The governor] chased all the market people away from that street," Samson adds. "And he said they have to rent shops to sell their goods. The shops cost 1.5 million naira ($4,760) to rent." I'm not sure if he means per month or annually. The average worker barely makes $300 per month.

Seyi takes over from Samson and continues to school me. There are millions of small traders in Lagos who live off the streets, who scrounge their daily living from passersby. According to him, barely a thousand banks operate in the entire city. Walkways like the planned one were clearing the way for a few hundred bankers' commutes, exiling millions of small entrepreneurs. Despite his exaggerations, I knew he had a point.

The government is moving traders to make the

streets cleaner and the city more organized, yet some traders feel they aren't being provided with affordable alternatives. They view the massive cleanups — filled with good intentions — as a way of making life a whole lot easier for the rich.

Lagos is a city riddled with half-solutions. Half-completed houses. Half-painted buildings. Half-tarred roads. Complete follow-through remains an elusive goal, at least to Samson and Seyi, as they argue beneath the tarp of their generator shop that afternoon. I watch their eyebrows arch angrily, sweat rolling down their faces while they debate their cause du jour. Earlier on, they'd been pondering why cars were driving in both directions on the one-way street with equal fervor.

But they have a point. The government is building a walkway that most traders would never see, let alone use, since they don't commute to offices, Seyi notes.

The vendor thanks my mother in Yoruba and I know an

agreement of some sort has been reached. He runs off to go find a light bulb, an electrician, and some diesel. Seyi and Samson join the other men lounging beneath the tarp to help lift the generator onto the paved street. My mother has demanded they test it right there and then.

We finally buy the generator at a relatively meager price two hours later, once we were sure it would work as advertised and delivery is arranged.

We walk back to our car, dodging the motorcycles and street vendors that swarm the sides of the street. At that moment, they seem quite a nuisance. We pass a lady selling sweet yeasty buns known as "poff poff," displayed in a heated glass box, probably priced at 10 naira (three cents) per bun.

I stare over my shoulder back at her.

There's no way she could rent a 1.5-million-naira stall to sell her *poff poff*.

Fijian Rose

Our white Volkswagen minibus hurtled down the gravelly mud road like an apparition against the indigo blanket of night. Besides the crush of heavy wheels against small stones and the thumping of hearts against ribcages, silence enveloped my colleague Andy and me. Anxiety had quelled our once-steady flow of banter. The occasional twig or branch slapped against the side of the bus and jolted us back into full alertness.

The only source of light — headlights illuminating two small misty circles ahead — showed the road converging into a narrower passage, which seemed more like a footpath. We startled as the first rain splashed against the windshield, almost tauntingly. Each subsequent drop exploded like a water-filled balloon.

Within minutes, the minibus nose-dived into a deep pothole, one of dozens that we'd soon face. Andy fought with the stick shift, changing gears, trying to climb out of the muddy pit. The minibus grunted in protest like a massive pig being pushed by an exhausted farmer into a small wooden pen. "Don't you know it," Andy joked, once it successfully lunged free. "We've got our very own jungle bus!" We made it out only to dip into another crack barely a 100 feet (30m) ahead.

We weren't lost. Markers had been placed along the way. All we needed to do was follow them as they drew us further into the depths of Viti Levu, Fiji's main island. Hours earlier, Andy and I had stared helplessly down at our boss Van like confused kids with a sick parent. Beads of sweat raced down his pale face as he lay, brought down by some violent stomach flu. We, his interns, had been given precise orders to drive to the remote village of Naivucini where the Eco-Challenge expedition race was scheduled to kick off at dawn the following day with dozens of adventurers gearing up to crisscross Fiji by land and sea.

Armed with nothing more than a roughly sketched map and enough bright-eyed enthusiasm to last weeks, we jetted off into the island's dark heartland.

So began a private expedition that saw us rolling past muddy rugby pitches where dark-skinned, shirtless men ran around clutching oval-shaped rugby balls stained brown from overuse. The same social scene repeated every couple miles down the road. A handful of little boys filed along the sidelines of each field, cheering at each beautifully executed tackle and jumping in eager anticipation of all the pickup rugby games that lay ahead for them in a matter of years.

Leaning slightly out the window, I soaked in the fresh breeze floating over from the Pacific Ocean, letting its revitalizing crispness course through me. We chuckled at the occasional fowl or stray dog darting across our path, but as semi-paved roads gave way to mud grooves, laughter morphed into uncomfortable silence.

A deep, dark fear rapidly gripped us and we braced for unfamiliar animals that might scurry across the narrow road as we pressed further into the dense rainforest.

Our hearts beat faster in excitement hours later as our circles of light finally illuminated other vehicles parked in a shallow roadside ravine. Smaller flashlight orbs then guided us towards the improvised campsite in a wet grassy field.

I hastily pitched my tent in the ink-black darkness, diving in fully clothed once it was barely up, afraid of what this opaque veil concealed. Rain pounded softly against the fabric walls in a soothing fashion. The island was rocking me to sleep, it seemed.

Come morning, the sun signaled her arrival, spilling through the tent's seams. I cracked open a small slot to finally peek at the world around me. Impenetrable, dark-green vegetation encircled the makeshift campsite. Country flags on wooden sticks were pegged into the ground, representing each racing team. Also dotting the landscape like wild mushrooms were thatched huts, known here as "bures." Village women in ankle-length flowery print dresses milled around, each sporting an oversized afro. Some rested a red hibiscus blossom in their thick curly nests of natural Melanesian hair.

Gravitating towards the soft choruses permeating the air, I found a cluster of women sitting cross-legged on the floor, making flowery leis.

"Bula (welcome)! My sister!" A woman I'd later call Rose leapt to her feet, recognition filling her eyes. She threw the handmade necklace over my head, eyes glassy with tears, welcoming me warmly into the very belly of Fiji.

Besides our different attire, I looked just like her and my fears of the unknown felt unwarranted.

The Reader in 26A

Beady eyes stared at me as I switched seats after takeoff from Lagos en route to Amsterdam. Our flight was barely full and yet a large, sweaty man was causing a scene, yelling at a flight attendant for not letting him move where he wanted to.

I watched my petite seatmate fumble for the remote control and I reached across her stack of books to help. Her long-sleeved sweater revealed narrow, fragile hands. "Oh, don't worry, my dear," she interjected. "I plan on sleeping all night. I'm just looking at it." I smiled back. A few seconds of silence.

"So where are you going?" I asked.

"Washington State to see my daughter," she replied. "I still have three more flights to catch once I get to Amsterdam."

"Washington State?" I gasped. "That's such a long way. How do you do it?"

"Don't worry. I slept for three days in preparation so I'm ready. If my child needs me, I hop aboard a flight. No questions." Each time, she leaves her village and makes her way down to Lagos — the bustling heartbeat of the country — to start the trip.

The woman and I began swapping flight check-in stories, commiserating about how we had to unpack and re-pack at the airport weigh-in.

"People are always asking you to buy them something. Please buy me this! Please buy me that! Like they actually gave you money to buy it," she added.

"So where are you going, my dear?"

"Sweden."

"Ha, Sweden. Isn't it one of those Scandinavian countries? Very cold with about 10 million people or so?" I nodded in agreement. "Next to Iceland, Norway, and what is that small country? Denmark!" she added. "I used to be a school principal, you know." She beamed. "And I love geography. Looking at maps and learning about the world."

"Very cool. So which other countries have you visited?" I asked, digging for more stories.

"Only the U.S. I can't go anywhere else, O!"

Our meals arrived and she immediately put away a bread roll for a snack during her six-hour layover.

"Didn't Roger Federer just beat that Swedish guy, [Robin] Söderling, in tennis?" she asked between mouthfuls. She looked at the plastic silverware and transparent food boxes, and then tucked those away too.

From my silence, she sensed my unasked questions.

"I read a lot. I read everything. After my husband died, reading became my comfort while my children are away."

She told me about her baby in college and how the older kids are chipping in to make sure she's cared for. They've had to since my seatmate hadn't received her pension in over 10 years. "Can you imagine?" she turned to me, her dark eyes shining like obsidian. "I've been to the ministry many times about the issue and the guy there wants to discuss the issue of my pension... something that's already mine."

Our conversation ebbed and flowed, sometimes diving into the country's cancer — corruption.

She lives in the Delta region where militants are fighting against the oil companies. They run rampant, kidnapping foreigners and breaking pipelines. Worse yet, opportunists have entered their fold. "Rogues are now joining the cause," she said. "That is the tragedy. The same with policemen."

She told me a story about a recent trip. Shortly after departure, policemen pulled over the crowded bus, seeking money from the passengers. They spotted her large suitcases and demanded to know who owned them. A passenger pointed to the lady at the back.

"Old woman! Are these your bags?"

"Didn't the other passengers already tell you?" she replied. The officer let out a dry laugh.

"Get off the bus, old woman!"

"Am I not free to sit on this bus?"

"You're too wise for yourself, old woman!" She stared

back at the officers, unflinching, not blinking.

"Are you a witch, old woman?"

Age isn't an exempting factor. It only determines the level of aggression they use.

We chatted for five of the six hours from Lagos to Amsterdam. We shared so many tales and anecdotes that need not be retold, but that I'll forever cherish. I was fascinated by this tiny woman: her experiences and her wisdom, not to mention her killer one-liners.

She tenderly adjusted her scarf over low-cropped white hair as I observed her.

"My name is Josephine," she finally introduced herself.

"I'm 71."

Notes on Zainab and Finding Talent in Corners

During a quest for traditional Nigerian artwork, I stumbled across Zainab's store. In a small corner of Lagos's Lekki Market (also known as "Jakande Market"), shoppers peruse sculptures, beaded necklaces, ceramics, and other decorative gifts at questionable prices.

"Questionable" because you need to start bargaining by taking half off right away.

But I was there to see a *mallam* (learned man) first and find treasures second. I'd been privileged to take this bead-seller's photo every time I'd visited the market over the last couple of years. So in my hand were several prints for him. His beard had grown lighter over the years, but his grin upon receiving the shots already filled my soul for the day. Eyes alight, he beckoned his son over and showed off the photos. Then he called across the alley to another vendor selling beads and displayed the images again.

I bought three necklaces from him. I didn't haggle or negotiate; I needed to move on and find those paintings I'd promised a friend back in Sweden. I pressed on, deeper into the market. I passed stalls selling almost identical wares: The market became a confusing maze until I rounded a corner. A green-patterned print pulled me in — bulbous flower petals etched into a traditional *ankara* (wax print) fabric — now stretched and molded into a handbag. I'd never wanted a piece of art more

in my life than at that moment. I longed not for the accessory, but for the beauty in the prints and their perfect arrangement.

That was when I met Zainab, creator of these bags.

She got me thinking about talent and passion, and about quietly laboring in your own corner. Battling upstream. Making a difference. Fighting off people who feel entitled to what you've labored to achieve. Building. Creating with your own hands. Working when frivolity continually seems to be rewarded and yet continuing twice — sometimes thrice — as hard.

I absolutely adored Zainab's eye and would love to see more people connect with her and her designs. I asked if she had a website, but she didn't — not yet anyway. Maybe she got just a handful of customers that day (myself included), maybe more. But that didn't dampen her resolve. She was put here to create and that she'll continue to do. Every single day.

So Zainab works away within her sphere of influence, developing beauty, creating art in her vibrant little corner of the world.

A piece of hers now rests in my little corner too.

WEST

Modena, Italy

Around 75,000 wheels of Parmigiano-Reggiano pass through the doors of Modena's 4 Madonne Caseificio dell'Emilia every year. Each is made from 600 liters (158 gallons) of organic milk from local red Vacche Rosse cows and black-and-white Holstein-Friesian dairy cows. Its member farms turn out 40 million liters (10.5m gallons) per year combined.

This adds up to one of the most impressive cheese-production machines in the world, accounting for two percent of all Parmesan.

This 1967 factory was visually jarring (in a very good way) for me as a photographer. I watched the wheels being manually tended to — flipped and rested in what I called a "baby-cheese nursery" — then soaked in brine for months and aged in batches of 33,750.

I happened to visit when quality control checks were being made by hitting each wheel with a hammer and gauging the audio feedback to assess if it were aging nicely or needed to be cast aside.

In my opinion, pure wizardry.

High Street

At 7am, the brass double doors open. First my black wheeled bag spills onto the wet pavement of London and then I follow. The doorman — gleaming in his freshly pressed scarlet uniform with gold trim — gives me a quick courteous nod and pulls the doors shut. The late February air is pungent with freshly fallen rain. This morning is darker than normal. Across the two-lane street — next to the large, sparse park — a heavyset woman with a thick dark-colored scarf waves frantically. As she tries to flag down a black cab, her face seems troubled.

Two fat pigeons startle me as they flap into my path, blocking me. "Who goes there?" they seem to ask, necks jerking left and right. They crane up to look at me, their rotund bodies remaining stationary. I detour around them, dragging my black bag. They remain unfazed and bend low to sip from the many puddles etched into the concrete pavement. I walk on. Opposite me, a two-storey red bus pulls up to a stop. Its light and warmth contrast sharply with the winter gloom. It appears very cozy with a handful of people heading to work that early Sunday morning. I long to be on that warm bus, but it speeds off the second it spits out a passenger to join me on my dreary walk.

I press on, past headless mannequins sporting spring collections in shop windows. I pause to study them. Draped around otherworldly proportioned bodies are silk dresses, soft cashmere sweaters, and tailored suits of expensive linen. The finest pearls loop around long lean necks. A jogger with a similarly otherworldly build whizzes by just as I turn to continue my walk. The only souls on foot are ours. Everyone else zips by in black cabs and the occasional lipstick-red double-decker bus.

Or so I thought as I startle two more souls tucked within an indentation bordered by three grey walls. They blow smoke lethargically, trying to warm up, despite sitting on wet concrete. The men say nothing to each other. I make eye contact with one, who stares back languidly. Not maliciously. But his resignation telegraphs: "I would normally say hello, but please forgive me, madam, I need a break."

I move on, the wheels of my bag splashing in puddles like a little kid. A bus pulls up not ten feet (3m) from me and my heart beats faster in anticipation of more kindred spirits joining me on this wet morning walk. A drenched woman steps out, swaddled in a thick brown coat over ethnic wear. The same look of resignation I'd seen on the cigarette-dragging men is plastered across her face. She glides off as quickly as the warm glowing bus.

Two blocks later, I reach my transition point. I steer left into the Underground station. I cruise past more headless mannequins. No sweet scents waft from cafes and bakeries for rushing people today. In fact, no people are rushing at all. Only two voices chat loudly at the end of the hall. Once I reach them, the more boisterous speaker helps me with my luggage as I struggle to get past the turnstile. "There you go," he beams. I thank him and make my way downstairs to the platform. I find two Japanese girls standing, not saying a word, waiting for the same train to Paddington.

Except it's never going to come. Not this Sunday morning anyway. A lanky guy in a navy-blue conductor's uniform gives us the bad news. Train service isn't running from here to the station just three stops away.

I turn back and lug my bag up the stairs. I pass the jolly gentleman who had helped me earlier, wondering if he'd already known about our plight. "Oh well," he replies genially and continues on with his banter.

I spill out onto the wet street once more, scanning for a warm black cab or a glowing red bus. Within seconds, a taxi travelling the opposite direction makes a sharp U-turn and waits for me. I hadn't even waved him down. I hurtle towards him, relieved.

"Paddington?" I ask.

"Yes, of course," he replies.

I hop into the toasty cab gracelessly, pushing my bag with the wheels in first and diving in after it. We sit in silence as he meanders along wet roads, heading towards more light, more life. There's nothing to talk about here.

London, it seems, is somewhere else.

From Manicures to Machu Picchu

My friends and I lay sprawled along the rocky narrow trail, utterly exhausted. With daypacks as pillows and sunhats half-covering our eyes, we had completely succumbed to fatigue. Our legs were failing us, muscles tensed from such unfamiliar, grueling exercise. My chest kept expanding wildly, trying to swallow as much of the thin air as it could. I'd done everything I was told to do, from drinking coca tea to chewing the plant's leaves to help with the high altitude. But even time-tested remedies wane as one's psyche takes over. Forging on was impossible at this point. I had mentally collapsed.

"Señoritas?" the voice started out low, gradually increasing in pitch as I stirred from my semi-conscious state. With wide grins, some toothless, a few Quechua porters stared down at us with a mixture of amusement and pity.

"Lo siento!" I managed an apology before rolling onto my side, making a wider space for them to pass on our narrow path. That didn't suffice. They wanted us to keep pushing on. We were carrying light daypacks, sporting the latest hiking boots, and wearing the coolest outdoor apparel. These pros were lugging an average of 60 pounds (27kg) of camping gear, climbing in rubber sandals made from old car tires.

We struggled to our feet, ashamed that we'd been ready to give up barely halfway through the trek. Day two on the Inca Trail found us stumbling 11 miles (17km) towards its highest point, Warmihuañusca — also known as "Dead Woman's Pass" — at 13,800ft (4,215m) above sea level.

With renewed vigor, we charged on.

No stranger to adventurous trips, I'd planned this renowned hike for months. My travels had already taken me from the remote dense jungles of Fiji and the Running of the Bulls in Pamplona to Jukkasjärvi way past the Arctic Circle in Swedish Lapland. This adventure was different. In addition to demanding physical endurance, it danced a mental tango with me, requiring that I reach deeper into my soul for strength.

During my adventures, finding people of color like me — who weren't natives — remained a rarity. Each time I spotted one, my face lit up like a child's. A close friend had once humorously noted that vacation meant relaxing on a sprawling white-sand beach, glaring as sun reflected off the cool turquoise waters of the Caribbean. Hoping to expand that perspective, I had invited friends of color on this challenge. Energized and excited, 20 said "yes," but our group quickly dwindled down to four when folks discovered an arduous four-day trek was in order.

The first day mentally pitted us against each other as we tried to match strides over eight rough miles (13km) of steep, rocky terrain. By day two, I finally decided to go at my own pace. Trying to complete the trek any other way seemed futile. The deceptive switchbacks made it feel like I was hiking around in circles with no end in sight.

Visibly disoriented and on wobbly legs, I was still first to reach our camp at Chaquicocha that night to applause from our porters.

After the grueling second day, the third day's undulating terrain felt more like a foot massage... Well, until we reached never-ending rocky stairs that threatened to take out our knees unless we appeased them by sidestepping. I pressed on, often trekking by myself for miles. In those precious moments — when time stopped and my mind was devoid of thought — I realized I was alive, listening to my breath, absolutely conscious and present in my life.

On the final day, I stood on calf muscles hardened from constant strain, waiting for the trail gates to open. Exhaustion had ravaged my body, but my mind focused on my destination, the Inca ruins of Machu Picchu. Aching pain and tense muscles seemed mild inconveniences at this point.

With our headlamps illuminating small circles ahead, we rushed past each other with no love lost, finally climbing steep stairs to the Cloud Gate. The last stretch had little to do with stamina. We had been reduced to basic primal emotions. The previous days of the strenuous journey had culminated at this point. "There it is! There it is!" trekkers shrieked. I put my glasses on.

And there she was... Machu Picchu.

By the hike's end, my friends and I had traversed jungles, rocky terrain, and summits over a span of 28 miles (45km). We'd walked amid and marveled at centuries-old Inca ruins such as Runkurakay and Sayacmarca. Tears of pain and joy fell. The air was thin and scarce, but at the end, we realized just how strong we'd always been.

The trail taught me two key lessons. First, the human spirit can withstand much more than we give it credit for, but more importantly, my race through life can only be completed at one pace — mine.

59

I Pledge Allegiance...

I watched my flustered friend Tito with amusement. She had the daunting task of selecting an outfit for her U.S. naturalization ceremony. She stretched a piece of ethnic wear — an *ankara* design (African wax print) — across her chest, then stared down at it and back up at me. We wrinkled our noses. We weren't sure it looked "American" enough.

I began to ponder. Do people lose a bit of who they are when they become citizens of a new country?

We worried that wearing traditional attire at a naturalization oath ceremony could jeopardize what was already hers — and that got me thinking. As you adjust to life in your new country, it becomes a daily struggle to hold onto your ethnicity as you try to seamlessly merge into a society that demands assimilation.

Tito's journey towards citizenship has been shared by thousands of Africans who immigrate to the United States, seizing opportunities that so many Americans take for granted. Some start on student visas that morph into working papers, which then crystallize into green cards. Others just win permanent residency in the green-card lottery or have to file asylum as a way of escaping crises and danger. No matter how diverse the journey's start, one thing always remains the same — the long process of courting the government.

Sacrifices must be made along the way. Often applicants have not been home in decades. Many can't even return if they wanted to. Families become distant entities on other continents. Only the emotionally strong undertake this process, knowing in the end that it may enrich their lives and their loved ones'.

But there is no guarantee.

As you near the end, you must be able to reaffirm that the journey itself and its perceived benefits were worth the struggle. If you cannot honestly feel this, you may have to abort this arduous, emotional task.

On Tito's big day, we arrived 30 minutes early to a hall with about six candidates, all casually dressed in western clothes. No one was wearing ethnic attire. My friend smiled at me. Maybe we'd made the right choice after all. But within seconds, we spotted an Ethiopian lady in a blue burka with her fingertips dyed black and henna designs snaking up her hands. Strolling in was an Indian woman in a peridot-green sari that clung to her gracefully.

We exchanged glances. Had we sold out too quickly? No sooner had that thought crossed our minds than attires began to flow in like Fashion Week in Paris. More burkas, traditional Asian prints, and a priest complete with a white collar. The final strut down the catwalk was an interesting mix of a black-and-white flowery mini-dress topped off with six-inch zebra-striped stilettos. The wave of diversity that hit us brought a point home.

The United States of America was built by immigrants and still draws strength from embracing them.

Finally a woman called "Ms. Comfort" walked in, making the biggest statement of all. Wearing a little black dress, she had strung across her shoulders a Ghanian kente wrap of bright, interwoven silk strips. The mix of both worlds spoke volumes: "I am here to stay and I am bringing my culture into your world."

She was Ghanaian and now she was also American, a right she'd worked hard to earn.

I looked at Tito's outfit — red jewelry, a white cotton shirt, and blue denim jeans — representing the flag. We didn't feel too bad after all. In this moment, she was embracing her new home. Today, she was American. She didn't have to prove her ethnicity by wearing her traditional attire. Ms. Comfort had testified to that fact.

Still, Tito vowed she'd wear ethnic garb tomorrow. She would always be Nigerian.

She too could be both.

Sweet Pillows

_____

"Lo! Cintra's glorious Eden intervenes, in variegated maze of mount and glen."
— Lord Byron, 1809

My host Rosa's warm brown eyes popped wide open like she'd seen a ghost. "You're going to Sintra?" she asked. I wasn't sure if it was a question.

Wasn't I supposed to go there?

The British Poet Lord Byron described this village as a "glorious Eden" in the early 19th century. Once the summer residence of Moorish lords and Portuguese kings, it's now a UNESCO World Heritage Site, celebrated as the first epicenter of European Romantic architecture.

Rosa was the day manager at a modest, two-room, family run hostel deep in the heart of Lisboa. Surely she must have been used to doe-eyed backpackers inquiring about Sintra, holding guidebooks with death grips.

I nodded weakly at her question. "Yes?"

"Please! You must bring me back a *travesseiro*. Please!" she spoke with such passion that I knew not fetching one, whatever it was, would be an injustice. She was born and bred in Lisboa, and if a local was asking for a *travesseiro*, it had to be worth finding.

I was seated over a simple breakfast of crispy wheat toast, orange marmalade, and coffee with her other lodgers. Zach, a rugged triathlete and dietician from Australia; Lisa, a youthful recent divorcee from the States; and Anna, a delicate New Zealander with a tumbling mass of soft brown curls. We'd been trading travel itineraries when Rosa happened upon our conversation, materializing the second I mentioned "Sintra," as if instinctively. Her reaction certainly intrigued my breakfast-mates.

"Sure," I responded.

"Ha! *Obrigada!* Thank you so much," she beamed and moved on as quickly as she'd entered into our banter. "Sounds like something we can't miss," Zach chimed in as he took a sip of black coffee. We locked eyes and I gave a half-chuckle. A few seconds of awkward silence followed. After all, we were but a foursome of strangers who'd just met the night before and were still feeling each other out — our best feet forward, followed by semi-formal chitchat.

"So..." I finally broke the silence. "Want to go find *travesseiros* with me in Sintra?"

64

We secured Rosa's directions to the exact *pastelería* (bakery). Detours to other sweet shops were strictly forbidden. Trying to source more information became a quest in itself. How would we know when we saw it?

"You will know."

At the Jardim Zoológico subway station, we found our connecting train to Sintra. The breakfast trio had ditched their day's plans to go on this intriguing chase with me. We made small talk as our train whizzed past the lush Iberian countryside. I'd stopped in Lisboa for three days en route to Spain, specifically Pamplona for the Running of the Bulls and to enjoy some reveling during the San Fermin festival. Lisa was heading to Italy to live for a while after her jaunt in Portugal, I found out. Zach was roaming the world for a year and was planning on a short working stint in London as a nutritionist after his travels. As for Anna, she just smiled shyly.

Sintra welcomed us with 19th-century pastel-colored castles against a blossoming backdrop of summer greenery. We found vividly restored cottages, grand palaces, elegantly aging water fountains, skillfully manicured lawns, and blooming gardens at every turn.

We seemed transported into Lord Byron's Eden. We spotted Moorish ruins crowning the hill and the sportsman among us pointed with longing. "Let's hike up there!" Zach announced with the same zeal Rosa had exhibited about her *travesseiro*. The hill seemed a challenge and being an Ironman triathlete, he needed to conquer it. Naturally, we had to join him on his quest, a clear detour from our task at hand.

I glared up at the steep narrow road to the palaces, then down at my flip-flops and knee-length jean skirt. I knew attempting a vertical ascent in my current garb was a tragedy waiting to happen.

I glanced at Lisa and Anna. Both were similarly dressed. A quick peek at Zach: He also sported thong sandals. Yet we all agreed to tackle the ascent, just as readily as the breakfast trio had dropped their day's plans for Sintra. Our need for belonging meant we would sacrifice to be seen as worldly, flexible backpackers.

Even in situations as mundane as climbing a sheer hill in rubber slippers.

But we did it anyways, and a few hundred feet into our ascent, we each began to pay the price in various ways. Our even pace became sluggish. Walking in short choppy steps due to my tight pencil-cut skirt, I started to lag underneath the weight of my army-green backpack.

Anna's freckled face flushed red and I wasn't sure if she was angry, tired, or both. But she didn't utter a word.

Zach turned back to assess the progress of the women. In the lead was Lisa with a steady one-two, one-two pace, followed by Anna using an unknown silent strategy, and then me beneath the rucksack. He rushed back down and reached for my bag.

"Please," he pleaded. Not because he wanted me to move faster, but because he'd felt a few pangs of guilt for the diversion and impromptu workout he'd inflicted on us. I bent my shoulder and the satchel slipped into his waiting arms.

"Thanks."

We continued up the winding road, taking in spectacular views of Portugal's sprawling scenery as we rounded each curve. Every painful step was rewarded with a striking and disarming angle of Sintra.

Ninety minutes later — fully drenched in sweat — we finally reached Castelo dos Mouros, the cliff-top Moorish ruins we'd spotted upon arriving in Sintra's heart.

Walking the grueling steps along meandering castle walls, we made out gray crumbling cisterns, battlements, and watchtowers dating as far back as 1147. The rich green Iberian countryside spread out around us in every direction, dotted with colorful little villages.

Over 850 years old, the walls still remained resilient and at that moment, our irritation with the hike seemed quite petty.

We pressed on towards the opulent Palácio da Pena, drawn by its pink and yellow façade like kids to a Technicolor lollipop in a candy store window. It was built in the 1840s, supposedly as a love nest for Dom Fernando of Saxe-Coburg Gotha and his wife, Queen Maria II. Every corner screamed "sumptuous" with a blend of Gothic, Egyptian, Moorish, and Renaissance elements in its architecture.

But we couldn't stay up there all day. Gawking at impressive ruins hadn't been our team's covert mission. Successfully lured off course by Sintra's beguiling charm, we needed to steer back on track.

We were still in search of Rosa's grail — *travesseiros*.

With blistered feet and worn out flip-flops, we headed back towards the punishing road. When we saw automobiles, Zach balked and voted to ride into town, a decision we all too gladly complied with. Our group flagged down a taxi, which whisked us straight into the now-jostling village center. Before dropping a few euros in our driver's hand, we asked about the *pastelería*. "Ha!" he gave us a knowing smile and pointed down a narrow, medieval side street.

We found Café a Piriquita unassumingly wedged in a corner. There was nothing particularly breathtaking about its look or ambience. However, a sweet smell of baked butter and sugar wafted from its interior, inspiring a long line of eager customers at its takeaway counter.

They were probably waiting for the very same thing we'd been deployed to find.

Twenty minutes later, all four of us were glued against the glass display. We scanned desserts oozing with fruit or savory fillings, pondering which had fueled our quest to Sintra. Defeated by our guessing game, I finally asked in pitiful Portuguese for a *travesseiro*. The young man behind the counter handed me a warm pillow-shaped pastry with a flaky crust and coating of sugar crystals. My companions each got one as well and we retreated to a secluded corner near one of Sintra's intricately carved fountains for the taste test.

At first bite, a rush of custard-like almond paste gushed into my mouth. Its juxtaposition of lightweight fluffiness and sugary decadence incited a euphoric feeling deep within me. One similar to what an awkward teenager feels when she finally discovers her high school crush had loved her all along too. It made sense that Sintra, in all its candy-colored glory, would produce something equally sweet.

I wanted more and couldn't get it down fast enough. We each devoured our pillows in gluttonous silence. Once I was done, I scanned my team. The look on their faces seemed a mixture of shock and bliss. I knew what they were thinking and decided to make it easier for us all.

"I could use another," I announced, trying to comport myself with some dignity.

"Yeah! Me too."

"Absolutely!"

We trekked back to Café a Piriquita to secure a couple more pillows, as well as two for Rosa. Standing in line didn't seem a nuisance the second time around. The anticipation of consuming the decadent pastry was enough to keep us waiting patiently.

With our newly acquired bounty in hand, we found our fountain once more and dug in. By the time we were done, us ladies had cleared roughly three each while Zach had polished off six *travesseiros* — each about two palms long. The only evidence left being a few sugar crystals at the corners of his mouth and a forlorn guilt-filled look on his face.

"What's wrong?" I asked, trying to pry out emotive details. How could an act so pleasurable bring on such a negative disposition?

"You don't understand," he started. "I had six of those. Think of all the calories. I'm a dietician. I know better."

He need not count calories, I tried reasoning with him. These pastries were a specialty and they needed to be savored in reverence. He let out a weak smile.

"Don't worry," I assured him. "No one has to know." This insatiable act would remain our foursome's dirty little secret...

We caught the train back to Sete Rios station, and started our walk down Avenida Columbano Bordalo Pinheiro with Rosa's now-cold *travesseiro* in hand.

"I've always wanted to try *caracóis*, you know, 'snails,'" Lisa shared as we strolled down the street, barely a few feet from the station. Interests were piqued once more, and Rosa's sweet pillow seemed a long-lost memory.

"Wanna go find *caracóis* with me tonight?"

Hanging with Cesenatico's Fishmongers

They had just brought in the morning catch from Italy's Adriatic Coast: thousands of varying fish and shellfish. Beneath tarps shielding them from the scorching summer sun, they sorted and cleaned crate upon crate of seafood.

Cesenatico's fishermen worked quietly and intently. They didn't banter much except for some forced jokes; I'd been spotted taking photos and they wanted to make me feel at ease. The preparation had to be done by the 2pm fish auction near the dock, where their fishing boats bobbed calmly in a canal harbor rumored to have been designed by Leonardo da Vinci himself.

I'm not sure how I developed my fascination with their trade, but I suspect growing up on Lagos's most famous barrier island, Victoria Island, had a part in it. I spent my childhood in close proximity to the powerful waves of the Atlantic Ocean. They lashed against Bar Beach, eating away its sand. I enjoyed exploring fish markets with my mom, buying mackerel, tilapia, and catfish for tomato-based stews. We fried tiny sardines for snacks, ate giant African snails, and sucked out periwinkles... I was surrounded by seafood and mollusks.

I've always been fascinated by what fishermen pluck from the depths, mostly because I've never been diving to see for myself. So fish markets are usually the first places I enquire about when I'm traveling.

The fishermen continued prepping with skill. Some crates were being loaded directly onto wholesale supplier trucks. Others were being ferried away into the auction's cylindrical building, the Mercato Ittico Cesenatico. Entering there, I felt like I'd stepped into a stock exchange of fish. Except there weren't people yelling or negotiating on the floor. Rather, they were perched in the auditorium-style rows of seats sloping towards the stage. The buyers chatted softly, poised over their buzzers. Crates of fish and shellfish came whizzing down the conveyor belt, only to stop in front of a Star Trek commander-style control center where the lead auctioneer was running the show and accepting bids. Above him a scoreboard showed who was bidding on what.

The standing auctioneers were a tag team; one chanting out the daily catch and vitals like weight, the other printing out the winning bid receipts and sending the crates down the conveyor belt to be picked up later. Cesenatico's fish auction runs Monday through Friday from 2pm. The vessels participate in a lottery determining who gets to sell their seafood first.

Amid the sea of middle-aged men, I met a vivacious soul — Jessica Quadrelli.

She spotted me and animatedly beckoned me over to join her and the guys. A group she clearly held her own in. Ripped biceps testified that she wasn't a stranger to hard back-breaking work. Jessica and her companions were curious about me, why I was there, and why I found

71

this seemingly mundane environment fascinating. Their positive energy was the only validation I needed.

For me, traveling and exploring deeply means discovering the things held dear by residents. What they feel is worth creating, building, doing. I respect the dignity passions bring, especially to people who use their hands daily like these fishmongers.

A photogenic seaside town in Romagna — between Ravenna and Rimini — Cesenatico celebrates its purported link to Leonardo da Vinci. One camp says he designed the canal in 1502, the other claims he just suggested improvements. Either way, it's a tie this small community holds on to like an anchor. The town itself dates back to 1301 when its harbor was dug and a defensive fortress was built. Today, Cesenatico is a thriving fishing community with a wholesale fish auction, historic fish market, and several independently owned *pescherie* (seafood shops).

Along the canal harbor stands the *Museo della Marineria di Cesenatico* (maritime museum) with historic wooden boats and other testaments to the town's important nautical legacy. It also doubles as an open-air exhibition, sheltering old fishing and cargo vessels with colorful patterned sails along its canalside docks.

A daily farmers' market flourishes in Cesenatico's center. En route to lunch, I picked up fresh cherries there among the charming little storefronts. I also visited traditional textile artists.

Lunch was at Pizzeria Nero di Seppia and featured platters of fresh sardines, octopus salad, and large prawns baked in salt. I dug into the *spiedini misto con verdure* (skewers of squid, shrimp, and vegetables) — my favorite meal during my entire stay in Emilia Romagna. I learned that Cesenatico holds an annual seafood festival each autumn, where over 70 regional restaurants showcase their specialties. For a bona fide seafood lover, this felt like a tease and I began immediately scheming to return.

Which leads me back to Jessica...

Roaming Cesenatico's narrow streets after lunch, I noticed La Piccola Pescheria della Jessica (Jessica's little fish shop). It didn't take long to figure out it was the very same woman I'd met an hour before at the auction. After all, the odds of finding many fishmonger "Jessicas" in a tiny community were pretty low.

She'd been at the auction during the early afternoon — when many businesses take a *riposo* (siesta) — to stock up on seafood for her ice displays. I now saw her winning bids being filleted, weighed, and wrapped in paper for her customers.

From the fisherman to the auction to her happy clients, I'd now seen the full, beautiful circle of Cesenatico's connection to the sea. The very reason I keep traveling slower to explore and experience a culture through its everyday lifestyles.

Waking up with Fishmongers

I wasn't expecting that smell of grease and batter frying in hot oil.

Oh, I did appreciate it but it certainly wasn't the briny overpowering stench of seafood smell I anticipated right away from a fish market.

Yet deep fry was the first scent that hit me as I strolled along Hamburg's harbor, where vendors were laying out fresh *fischbrötchen* (buns filled with herring). Massive cruise ships rested in the background like sleeping giants under the early morning's blue light. The market's lamps guided me — and some late-night partiers — down a makeshift alley of stalls selling fried mackerel, smoked salmon, pickled herring, and cooked prawns.

I wandered past a few stalls until I struck that now-familiar pungent smell of sea salt and fresh fish interspersed with fast-food kiosks. Further along lay a sea of vibrant fruit and flower hawkers with neatly arranged baskets. This was clearly more than an assembly of fishmongers.

Hamburg's historic Fischmarkt (fish market) is held at the crack of dawn every Sunday morning between March and November (5am usually, but 6am in winter). Running since 1703 along the Elbe River's banks, it was crowned by the Altona auction hall in 1896. Over the years, the fish market has morphed from a sweat-it-out haggling ground for fishermen, fishmongers, and customers to a place that draws thousands of tourists — roughly 70,000 every year — with business still being conducted amidst it all. Bands even play jazz, country, and rock music as patrons dig into all manner of fish for brunch.

Styled like an industrial Roman basilica, the Fischmarkt has burnished red brick walls and a dome roof made of steel and glass. It was inaugurated by Kaiser Wilhelm II and remains the city's waterfront icon.

There is a clear difference in clientele at 5am versus 6am, I discover. In that crucial hour, locals call dibs on the freshest fish and seafood. They rub shoulders with revelers who stumble out of the hedonistic St. Pauli quarter and off the Reeperbahn, looking for early morning grub and coffee. Then the market is most alive and true to form. And of course, it rewards those of us who roll out of bed to soak up the lively vibe with cameras in hand.

Matching the fish merchants are scores of fruit and vegetable vendors, in case you want to gorge on something healthier in the wee hours of the morning. So while some hungover clubbers maintain death grips on seafood sandwiches, others carry baskets of apples, bananas, oranges, pineapples, grapes, and coconuts, just to name a few.

Oftentimes with a bottle of beer in the other hand...

When it comes to over-the-top personalities bellowing from their stands, the market certainly doesn't disappoint. For example, Dieter Bruhn — nicknamed "Eels-Dieter" — has been in the business for over 50 years. This "Godfather of Fish" is one of the defining fixtures of the modern market. Rounding a turn, I catch him from the corner of my eye. All-knowing. All-seeing. All-hearing. He wears red suspenders, a white turtleneck, and a navy-and-white striped shirt with sleeked-back hair. Dieter is so influential that Hamburg's official website has dedicated a page to him.

And then there is Michel, blasting reggae and churning out cup after cup of coffee. "*Lecker lecker* (yummy yummy)," he shouts. "*Lecker lecker!*" And then "quality, not quantity."

His verve and patter instantly injects visitors with adrenaline, despite the early hour. He sparks me awake. Alert. Excited and ready to explore more of the market... but only after reluctantly prying myself away from his side.

I know his melodic chant will be forever ingrained in my mind.

The traditional fish vendors remain. Amidst the bustle and energy the other merchants were giving out that threatened to dwarf them.

Yet they endure as the cornerstone of this historic trading place, which truly is worth getting up at 4:30am to experience.

Notes on Marriage, Space, and Travel from Paco

The driver glanced at me through the rearview mirror. Paco wanted to make sure I was comfortable. Or as comfortable as I could be at 11pm while traveling from the airport to downtown Toronto twinkling in the distance.

"Is everything okay, ma'am?" he asked.

"Yes, thank you," I responded, but I wasn't sure he heard across that distance. Honestly, I'd rather have sat in the passenger seat than what felt like 10 feet (3m) away, hugged by soft dark leather in his luxury sedan.

"Where are you from?" he asked. I told him that same old story starting with Lagos, transitioning through the U.S., and then settling in Sweden.

After my teenage and young adult years in the States, I consider myself Nigerian-American, as well as Nigerian.

Originally from Mexico, Paco had been here for at least 15, maybe 20 years. He loved his adopted country Canada and had traveled around it quite a bit. "My cousin is moving to Vancouver and I'm looking forward to visiting him out there too," he said, before carefully switching lanes. "That area is known for skiing as well," he ventured.

"I've tried it only once," I said. "And it reminded me why I'm African. I didn't like it and it felt quite unnatural for me to be skiing down the side of a mountain for fun."

He laughed loudly.

"You know, I've also been skiing but I didn't like it either. My friends warned me to

79

take some pain-relief medicine before I went. I didn't. The next day, I was so sore I couldn't move. I'm Mexican. Just give me a soccer ball and I'm happy," he shared.

I laughed loudly.

"So I take it you love to travel and try new things?" I asked.

"Oh, I love to travel," he beamed. "I traveled a lot before I was married and now that I'm married with children, I still get to travel. I just got back from Peru. Alone."

"Alone?"

"Yes, just give me a backpack and I'm off. I love being spontaneous. I explored Lake Titicaca. I went to Machu Picchu. I couldn't hike there because the trail was closed, so I took the train. But it was amazing," he continued.

"That's wonderful," I said. "So how often do you get to travel every year by yourself?"

"Well, my wife and I started our own little thing... at each one's birthday, you get to go off somewhere on your own and do what you love. So she can go off with her girlfriends and do whatever she wants. For my birthday, I get to travel solo, and explore and enjoy the things I want to," he replied.

Downtown Toronto was getting closer. I wanted to push it back a few more miles.

"So for me, it was Peru this year. Next year, maybe a safari in Africa."

"I love this," I said. "Because it lets you be who you were before you got married. And it's so easy to lose one's self once marriage and kids come."

"Exactly! And doing it around our birthdays gives us the time to reflect alone on just how far we've come individually without losing the core of who we are," Paco said. "I'll always be a traveler. My wife knows and understands this."

I'd always known just how important this space to be you within marriages was and I'm also extremely grateful for a spouse who understands and supports me. But it made my heart soar hearing this from Paco — especially the birthday aspect, giving each other space to muse and celebrate personally. Yes, they had kids, but they made it work in a way that strengthened their relationship.

I didn't need to tell Paco that I'd also been to Peru or that I'd been fortunate to hike four days along the Inca Trail to Machu Picchu.

It didn't matter.

The Sicilian Countryside

Arriving around 8pm, my husband Urban and I boogied to some '80s tracks at a random happy-hour event we stumbled into at the hotel, before getting out of Palermo the very next day. This trip certainly wasn't about museums, sightseeing, hitting Sicily's famous beaches, or gluttonously gorging on pizza. It also wasn't about getting off the "beaten path" — so to say — with an itinerary of activities in hand.

Considering tickets were purchased and hotel reservations made barely a week before departure, we knew we had to go with the flow to avoid unnecessary stress. And so, it really was about hopping into a rental Peugeot hatchback and seeing where Sicily chose to take us... despite the GPS unit.

And boy, did the island take us deep into her interior, through the Madonie Mountains along harrowing cliffside roads to the relatively remote village of Gratteri. There we would unplug and hide out for three days, wandering empty single-track streets and hearing the occasional lady yell in Sicilian Italian across a clothes-strewn balcony to her neighbor. Most of Gratteri's 1,000 inhabitants were away and so we had the farming village to ourselves... along with old men and their walking canes who gathered every evening at their watering hole — Bar La Villa — to eat gelato, drink coffee, and talk boisterously.

They never tired for gist on a daily basis as we greeted

them with "*buon giorno.*" I always wondered what they chatted about. What they've been chatting about for decades. The same stories, I reckon, from different angles. We did gorge on pizza topped with salty prosciutto and the freshest gorgonzola cheese in Gratteri. Because here in our off-the-travelers-track find, a small car winds through narrow roads to home-deliver bread, the vegetable guy rolls his truck through town every couple days, the main square consists of four gelato kiosks that moonlight as bars, and no one can order pizza until the pizza guy comes.

We continued along Sicily's touristy coastline hitting Cefalù, Milazzo, Taormina and Giardina, but we constantly missed Gratteri for the rest of the trip. Ditching our car for two days, we ferried over to the Aeolian Islands to see Stromboli occasionally spurt lava. The islands rewarded us with seven shooting stars in a single sparkly night. Eyes locked, we beamed shyly, falling in love all over again. Barely three days later, after we left Lipari, a 4.5-magnitude earthquake would injure a handful of people and cause several rock slides, bringing us back to earth once more.

Our serendipitous journey gradually wove down to Greek-influenced Siracusa, a city stamped across the sprawling countryside. Here we dug into whole squid, fresh fish, and fist-sized prawns in Ortygia, before searching for more Baroque splendor in Noto and Ragusa. Deep within this hilly province, snaking across mountainous switchbacks, ours was the only car in sight. We gaped silently in reverence at 14-mile (22km) stone walls, listening to the sounds of cow bells. Here we found a softer side of Sicily.

Away from suntanned barely clad crowds, distracting technology, and constant ambient noise, we remained fully aware of each other and are now much closer for it.

The Terracotta Life

The road to Ville Montetiffi snakes along rolling Italian hills with lush views of green vineyards, fields with grazing sheep, and farmland with old sheds and villas. Past the occasional cyclist training and struggling uphill. Past a car or two, few and far between. In the distance, you can just make out the microstate of San Marino dramatically jutting from the mountains. For long stretches, mine was the only car on the road as I pressed further up into Emilia Romagna's Sogliano al Rubicone province. There was no cellular coverage here. Montetiffi required that I fully immerse once I reached her.

I was on my way to a rustic farm, where for decades the Camilletti-Realis have been reviving the over 500-year-old tradition of handmaking terracotta pans. Rambo, the family's dog, barked our arrival and Rosella came out to meet us with a smile, her eyes twinkling. Maurizio was spinning his lathe in the workshop, finishing up a pan, fingers dyed brown with clay.

They are the only artisans keeping alive the clay pans called *"teglie"* within this region. Italians use these to cook *piadina* (flat bread) made with wheat flour, lard or olive oil, salt, water, and a pinch of bicarbonate or yeast. It can be eaten with cheese and cold cuts like prosciutto or Parma ham as a sandwich or with sweeter fare such as Nutella and jam or ricotta cheese topped with caramelized figs. The bread is certified a *"prodotto agroalimentare tradizionale"* (protected regional food product).

Disillusioned with the daily grind, the married couple bought their farm in Ville Montetiffi years ago and learned how to make *teglie* from an old potter to help preserve the dying tradition. Today, they're the only producers in the area, selling to small stores, as well as at artisan fairs.

Maurizio showed me some raw materials — red and blue clay, as well as marbled calcites — that he uses to make the pans. I watched the artist take his place at the potter's wheel, his hands gently shaping and crafting a *teglia*. His honey-colored eyes scan the surface like lasers for any imperfections and his fingers swiftly correct the single one he finds. Because he's been doing this for roughly two decades, the rotating wooden lathe feels like an extension of his body.

Within minutes, a perfectly smooth flat pan was molded and ready to dry under the shade in the evening sun. The semi-dry teglie are then transferred into a storage room where they set for seven to eight weeks with regular rotations, before being baked in a wood-burning kiln. This long process reaps its full benefit after close to two months.

But that was expected. Because here in the hills — away from the beach crowds in Rimini or bustling students in Bologna — slow living was essential to one's craftsmanship as an artist. People worked with their hands in a way that required full concentration. This was a life I envied on some level. One which would mean

substituting what I constantly pursued with what I truly needed to live a less stressful lifestyle. The life of an artist who drew inspiration from his surroundings and who relied on them to recharge his creativity.

Beyond their craft, Maurizio and Rosella also live off the land in a sustainable and rustic way. After I accepted their invitation to join them for dinner, he went out to pick black cherries and fresh strawberries from his farm, as well as green leafy vegetables for a salad. They get cheese and dried meats from neighbors down the road, who maintain small holdings too.

Tonight, Rosella invited me into her warm kitchen to teach me how to make piadine from scratch. Their 14-year-old son Francesco was in the background playing a video game on their computer. His mother measured out flour as a kettle of water whistled steam in the background. She mixed it with salt, lard, and bicarbonate before kneading the dough into its familiar consistency. She had been making flatbread from scratch for close to 20 years — and her skills shone.

Dinner was simple but hearty. We ate the *piadine* with fresh salad tossed with salt, olive oil and caramelized figs that Maurizio had made himself, alongside ricotta, parmesan cheese, and a variety of cold cuts. I listened mostly, upset that I couldn't converse in Italian. After all, when I was a teenager, I'd spent at least two years teaching myself the language. But it didn't matter now as we chatted over dinner with Nicholas: my guide, friend, and impromptu translator. Upon finding out my nationality, the Camilletti-Realis told me about a Nigerian friend of theirs called "Friday" who lived down the hill. I wondered if Montetiffi — pretty much the antithesis of life's maddening rush in my hometown of Lagos — had also seduced him as well with the ultimate calm.

I listened. Because if I talked, I couldn't trust myself not to cry. Mostly because of the warmth, genuine

hospitality, and love that surrounded that table. I saw a tiny piece of my own decision to leave the cutthroat corporate world reflected and validated in their artisan values. Life was truly meant for living in a way that didn't necessarily mean amassing wealth one can never spend.

As Maurizio walked us to the car, the sun was setting over Montetiffi up on a distant hill. He paused and took in its golden rays, washing over the landscape that spread all around us.

"I never get tired of seeing this after all these years," he said.

EAST

Phnom Penh, Cambodia

While traveling through Cambodia as a photojournalist with a non-profit organization, I decided to visit the World Heritage Site Wat Phnom (Hill Temple) with its resident monkeys on one of our days off.

As macaques of varying sizes scurried around interacting with guests, I noticed they were being fed snacks and fast food. A man even walked up to a monkey and handed it a can of Fanta, which the animal started downing like sweet nectar from the gods.

I took the shot.

In terms of composition, it's one of my favorites for the human-like body language and expression of absolute enjoyment on the monkey's face. But the image also distresses me because macaques shouldn't be cooling off on hot and humid days with Fanta. In fact, many of the monkeys grew sick and violent towards tourists, and were relocated by the Phnom Tamao Zoo and the Forestry Administration in 2011.

As travelers, our actions can negatively live on long after we move onto the next destination.

My Polish Informant

September 2003.

Our party bus crosses the border into Poland from Slovakia. We're pulled aside and a control officer hops on. He glides down the aisle, sucking air and grabbing passports. He must love his job.

He reaches me and pauses, pinning me to the leather seat with a glassy blue stare. I slip my worn, forest-green Nigerian passport into his long, lean hand. He flips through green-tinted pages and studies the unfamiliar document.

"It's a passport!" my inner voice yells. It has already screamed twice earlier today. I could go hoarse easily at this rate.

Grabbing the foreign item from me, he slides it beneath the stack of blue (U.S.) and red (E.U.) documents already in hand. He needs easier access, I tell my American seatmate. The official grabs her navy passport and places it atop the pile.

He hops off the bus and summons a colleague. Draws his attention to that forest-green book. Ten noses press against glass windows like school kids', as my companions observe their interaction below.

"Uh-oh! Lola is in trouble again!" my friends chant. I smile. They pull me back into the fold, but the officers win the tug of war. The first official signals for me to disembark. I need to explain that green book in person. This will mean arriving into Kraków later than anticipated.

The city is quite sexy beneath the veil of night. I wasn't expecting her to be. She senses my dejection and steers us underground to Club Fusion with its labyrinth of lounges carved from rock; its magenta, cyan, and yellow strobe lights.

Hip hop night. I check out the dancing Poles. I feel out their vibe. I proceed to a corner to dance... and dance and dance until a man approaches me, covered in black.

Tall. Head shaven. Eyes similar to those that had pinned me to my seat earlier that evening, demanding I explain what I wanted in his country... and from his country.

We dance silently for 15 minutes.

"Michal," he finally introduces himself. I nod weakly. I want nothing to do with him. We dance some more. He studies my face. I turn away.

"Where are you from?" he asks. I tell him about my green passport.

Blue eyes now dyed red from the strobes light up in recognition. He grabs my hand and pulls me forcefully. He drags me through underground caves. We sail through masses of sweaty people.

He plants me squarely in front of a group leaning against a wall.

I study their faces. My countrymen. "These are my friends!" he introduces. I turn to Michal. The words never come but he hears them anyway.

He grabs my hand and gives it a kiss.

A Convergence at Sue's

Cryptic Magyar text — etched on aging brown walls and modern signposts — guides my husband and I down stony narrow paths that snake through Belváros in Pest, Hungary. We meander in search of dinner, following the scent of sweet Viennese pastries, salty cheese-laden aromas of baking pizzas, and whiffs of slow-grilled kebabs down dark alleys. The choices seem endless, even at this near-witching hour, as one fragrance distracts us from the next with alluring hints of spices.

More decisive diners sit at candlelit windows, yet we press on, still certain we will find the epitome of late-night chow. We stroll along the river, the Danube herself now a still, dark mirror reflecting sparkling lights of the Buda district high above us.

Now one scent dominates: a mixture of chili and basil. We gravitate towards a dimly lit Thai restaurant, pushing open glass double doors to the chiming of bells. Rows of plush velvet chairs and dark mahogany wooden tables stand empty, save for one. Seated around it are six men dressed in casual attire. They talk technology with a mix of American, British, and Australian accents over plates of half-eaten fried rice and stir-fries. We make our way to the counter where an older Thai man in his fifties talks on the phone.

"*Hellosztok!*" another voice greets us in Hungarian from behind the counter and we crane to find its source. Within a split second, a woman is standing at my side and peering up at us through dark eyes. The mix of Anglo-Saxon accents negotiating business becomes muffled background noise.

"Where you from?" she demands before we attempt to order.

"Sweden," my husband answers.

Nigeria by way of America, I reply.

"Ha! I live in New York, you know," she switches into American English tinted with a Thai accent. "I spend a month here every year." While we process her information, she continues. "I am Sue! How did you two meet?" Before we answer, she enquires about our order for the night.

She scribbles down cursive Thai symbols and passes the note over to the chatty man. He disappears into the back room.

For 16 years her family has run this place, Sue tells us, through tight-fisted communist regimes to the present-day parliamentary rule. Theirs was among the pioneering set of ethnic restaurants that now freckle Budapest. Permanently living here didn't seem like the

best option to Sue. This freedom she had — to roam the world and move seamlessly between cultures — was something she held on to for dear life.

Barely 10 minutes later, the man returns with two oil-stained brown paper bags. He hands them over without a word and continues back to his spot by the phone.

Sue walks us to the door and before we leave, I turn to her.

"*Köszönöm szépen,*" I attempt a thank you, my delivery inelegant. She lets out a high-pitched laugh.

"Pleeease!" she says, placing her hand on my back. "Sixteen years and I still can't speak Hungarian."

Trafficking Innocence

I choked on my chicken curry when Boupha* told me she was 12.

She looked six.

Unlike Western countries where preteens may appear old enough to drive, the reverse was the norm in Cambodia. Despite their youthful appearance, these girls had been forced to grow up quickly, living through inhumane conditions within brothels and experiencing situations children are never supposed to even witness. I was traveling as a volunteer photojournalist with an anti-sex trafficking team to Cambodia and nothing could have emotionally prepared me for my most challenging trip to date.

Our group had spent the better part of the morning with 21 girls, ranging from five to 16 years old, at a secure assessment center. We'd observed them singing, dancing, and creating art and crafts. Now we were getting to know them personally over a simple, yet hearty, lunch of white rice and yellow curry.

Earlier on that hot, humid November day, I had ridden in a *tuk-tuk* (three-wheeled vehicle) with a program officer. A spirited Filipino man, he explained the rescue organization's operations in a tone heavily laden with optimism. The high-security abode acts as a refuge for girls who had been raped, kidnapped, or sold as sex slaves and prostitutes. They reside here until their initial legal battles are over. Subsequently, they are either transferred to a shelter or returned home if their families are deemed safe enough to protect them. The center provides short-term care such as medical checkups, mental evaluations, and family assessments for the first two months of rescue before transfers to other more permanent shelters. We were fortunate to get behind those secured gates.

Cambodia has roughly 15 million residents and ethnic Vietnamese comprise at least eight percent of the population. Yet half of the girls rescued annually are of Vietnamese decent. We'd planned to spend time with them decorating rubber flip-flops with ribbons, stickers, colorful beads, feathers, and sparkling press-on jewels. This provoked shrieks of excitement and quickly reminded us that innocence and joy could survive even horrific conditions. The little girls were grabbing at pink, purple, and pastel accessories. The rest of that humid afternoon was spent blinging out sandals, as well as making bracelets and painting faces. Even though it seemed a mundane project, it allowed them to be kids once again.

As the day wore on, one of the girls, who was mute,

became more energetic and broke out of her shell. I wondered if she'd been born silent, which eventually led to her being sent to a brothel, or if she'd been so severely traumatized that not talking was a defense mechanism — a way to cope with her ordeal.

As they played, I observed these kids. Deep dark eyes. Strong jawlines. Flawless skin. They ranked among the most gorgeous children you could ever meet, and I constantly had to remind myself of what they had been through within those brothels.

Later in the week, I visited one of the more permanent shelters in Kampong Cham, a province close to the border of Vietnam. Thousands of girls — estimates say 800,000 — are trafficked from Vietnam through this

province every single year. Driving down backroads along the Mekong River, we finally reached our destination a couple hours later. Beautiful traditional singing welcomed us. The difference in the girls' dispositions at the shelter in Kampong Cham and those at the assessment center was night and day. These girls were filled with sanguinity and had begun to adjust to the normalcy of life outside a brothel. They'd started learning vocational crafts, as well as attending school once again. This time around, these girls were the first to extend hugs to us foreigners.

"It takes a certain type of person to be a private investigator," explained Sam, an undercover detective who had surveillance teams dispatched all over Southeast Asia. Our group met with him over lunch in Phnom Penh a few days later. "One has to go into brothels, act like a customer, and put themselves in awkward and morally challenging positions to rescue a girl."

With years of criminal investigation under his belt in his native Australia, Sam moved to Southeast Asia to combat the epidemic of human trafficking with an estimated 1.2 million children affected each year in the region. Organizations such as UNICEF, Save the Children, World Vision, Chap Dai, World Hope, and the International Justice Missionary are just a few actively fighting the issue. There are no shortages of NGOs based in Phnom Penh that fan out into the most remote of regions within Cambodia to help educate villagers and fund community development projects as alternatives to selling children for income.

As I watched Boupha scoff down large spoonful's of rice yellowed from mixing with curry, grinning between mouthfuls, humility washed over me. In her mere six years, she had witnessed how low man can go... but also how high we can rise back up. And she was still smiling.

*Names have been changed to protect the subjects.

Kwang Yaw

A sharp turn off the paved main road and our volunteer team finds itself plowing through muddy, unpaved tracks dozens of miles from Phnom Penh, Cambodia. Bustling city activity and buildings are quickly replaced with seas of lush, green rice fields. Worn-out street bicycles replace motorbikes. We crane every which way, taking in the tall palm trees that rise starkly from the paddies. It is early morning and farmers are already tending their crops. We spot a few fishermen on long canoes, crossing the shallow swamplands.

Glancing starry-eyed at each other, we take it all in.

We are visiting the only primary school for miles and are bearing face paints, balloon animals, egg-shaker instruments, and a couple soccer balls for impromptu games. Eager anticipation fills our modest van. We are looking forward to working with the kids, ranging in age from six to eight. We hope to connect with them through crafts they have probably never seen or heard of before.

The road becomes more challenging to navigate. Straw huts and homes on wooden stilts begin to emerge as we near our destination. Seconds from the school, a face-off ensues with the children. In little blue-and-white uniforms, they dot the landscape like strewn pieces of candy. They stare at the van as if it were an apparition, and then dart into their schoolyard once they realize what is happening. Giggles and small scampering feet welcome us as we disembark. They epitomize cuteness.

107

Meandering from classroom to classroom, I observe volunteers at work, making balloon animals and painting wee faces. Furiously shaking their new, plastic musical instruments shaped like Easter eggs, the kids begin to sing and scream in tiny, yet shrill, voices. I beam and scan each child until I finally spot him. He grins at me with a giant smile with a gap between his two front teeth.

He is absolutely precious and I instantly consider him my son.

We stroll into the nearby village, where a wave of life and smells overcomes us. We step back into a time where living simply is all that really matters. Beneath stilt homes lie pens of livestock. From sows and piglets to ducks and ducklings, and chickens and chicks, animal husbandry is one of the residents' main sources of sustenance. Cattle wallow under tarps and observe us, the approaching intruders. Vegetable gardens emerge as we press deeper, and enormous heads of the freshest lettuce grow from fertile land.

"Or Kun," we thank the elders gleefully as they grant us permission to explore their village. They sense our excitement and lower their heads slightly in response. Children's laughter fills the air and we gravitate to the source, only to arrive at the edge of the lake.

Wooden canoes line its banks. The kids swim with reckless abandon in its murky green waters. Some try to use their balloon animals as flotation devices. The little boys do back flips and cannonballs off the sterns of canoes, making splashes as loud as their small bodies can. I spot my "son." He peers out at me, neck deep, and gives me a wide grin before disappearing beneath the surface like an alligator. I beam proudly.

We stroll by village women playing a card game, men swinging lazily in hammocks, and older villagers trying to decipher how we got here – and why. It is time to head back to the school and we leave the village like pied pipers with a swarm of kids trailing. They are still eager to show us every inch of their village.

More balloon animals are made and faces painted that afternoon. The little boys begin exchanging their inflated swords for air-filled flowers. Our norms mean nothing here. Appreciating the simplest of things is what sums up one's existence in Kwang Yaw. We quickly realize the unlimited bounds of energy that first- and second-graders possess; keeping up seems futile.

Several hours later, it is time to go. The humid air feels denser. Our bags seem a couple pounds heavier. Tiny pattering feet shadow large, heavy ones as we stroll back to our van. The ride back to Phnom Penh is somber. The lush green fields don't seem as captivating anymore. Even the beauty of the gorgeous floating lotus flowers begins to wane.

Certain sadness fills me. I have left my son behind.

Slow Traveling through Markets

I was waiting at the still-closed gates around 5:45am. Fishmongers lined the stone walls, sitting on plastic chairs, wooden stools, and doorsteps. A cigarette gently balanced between fingers. The click-swish of a newspaper page being turned. A yawn, then a stretch rippled here and there.

They were waiting. Waiting for freshly caught fish from the Adriatic Sea to be delivered.

I settled in with them, sometimes flashing a grin. After all, I didn't speak any Croatian beyond basic greetings. Sometimes I lightly conversed in English with those who could, but mostly I just waited in companionable silence. They knew why I was there. After all, I had my professional camera resting on my hip like a baby — incredibly obvious despite being beneath my scarf. I wanted to be a fly. They needed to know this. A nonintrusive fly.

Once the door flung open, the dizzying rush filled the early morning air, redolent of scraped fish scales, mollusks being cleaned, and the sorting of mussels and clams: the heavy pungence of aquatic death. I pressed myself against a wall, slowly gliding along, observing. I stayed out of their way, only lifting my camera on intuition. After all, this was their most important time of the day. The fishmongers needed to present their

seafood in a desirable fashion to court customers. I observed enough to catch their rhythms and how they moved. I slid in sync when I needed to take a photograph — never obstructing their views or interfering with their work. But I did interact during downtimes, asking about their morning, their work. Then I retreated as the rush resumed...

I'm an advocate for slow travel. I don't feel the need to race through places as quickly as I can. This also means that if I have a few hours or days in a place, I usually focus on one activity or deep-dive into a theme as best as I can, truly exploring the culture.

I've stopped keeping bucket lists, though I still want to fearlessly explore the world and expend my wanderlust. Rather, I quit counting countries and checking off experiences because, the older I've gotten, the more I've realized that travel isn't a race to be won. For me, moving through the world means listening to and experiencing the lifestyles of its people.

To listen, one needs to pause.

The concept of slow travel sounds misleading at first, because people automatically equate "slow" with time spent in a place. Arguments against slow travel range from it being unrealistic for full-time

workers to borderline pretentious, especially within the never-ending debates over "tourist" versus "traveler." But you don't need weeks or months to immerse. I have a young family and spending ages away to inch through a region would mean I'm not setting my priorities right. And truthfully, most people don't have the luxury of four to six weeks off work, let alone a nomadic lifestyle that allows them to wander indulgently.

But to me slow travel has never been about duration. It is about pace. It encourages us to relax and reconsider why we're traveling. It inspires us to embrace seeing less, but going deeper into a culture — and how that can enrich and transform us much more than skimming its surface.

I connect with a place through its local lifestyles, regardless of whether I'm spending 24 hours or 24 days there. In a city, that could mean lingering in a particular district with a certain group of people. I most like to hang out with butchers, fishmongers, and fruit and vegetable vendors.

I was able to get the lifestyle shots I wanted before the Split fish market kicked off at 7am for residents and tourists alike. Once the doors officially opened, I saw other cameras coming, aimed straight-on before ever getting to the fish vendors' tables. Almost like drawing one's weapon immediately. It instinctively and subconsciously puts up a wall between the subject and the photographer.

If only they'd come a few hours earlier to spend some time bonding and appreciating the work the sellers do. Acknowledgement goes a long way and letting people know you're willing to wait alongside them before their work begins speaks volumes.

Even if you're waiting in silence with no shared language.

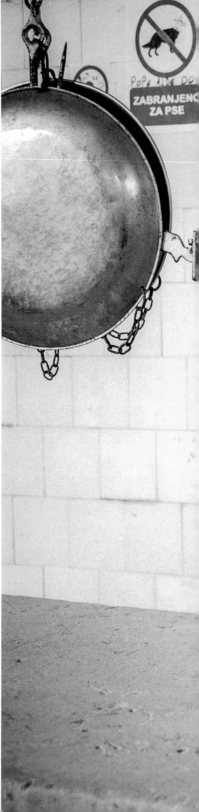

NORTH

Gulf of Bothnia, Sweden

The northernmost arm of the Baltic Sea is one of the most underappreciated regions of the country. It is quicker to hop on a plane and fly an hour to Luleå instead of undertaking a 12-hour road trip from Stockholm. But that long, grueling drive weaves you past tranquil landscapes.

Classic red-and- yellow cottages alongside pine trees. Still lakes reflecting wide blue skies and low-hanging clouds, caked with snow like sugar frosting during winter. Colorful rowboats docked alongside wooden piers that run into small bays just off the Gulf of Bothnia.

During the coldest, darkest months, the sun hovers over the horizon but never truly rises.

Port of Call

I recognized those haircuts from 1987, almost 30 years ago.

Complete with tapered stonewashed jeans tucked into high-top sneakers, teenagers and young adults filled the decks. This was, I presumed, going to be their weekend booze cruise. The next demographic up were middle-aged men with forlorn looks, dragging at cigarettes, followed by families with kids under ten years of age.

I was embarking on my first cruise ever and observing its patrons sure beat people-watching at the airport.

The proximity of my home city, Stockholm, to major Baltic capitals like Riga, Tallinn, and Helsinki brings an international flair to short jaunts. Ferries depart daily from Frihamnsterminalen in the afternoon and return mid-morning two days later. Our vessel sailed away promptly at 5pm, Stockholm fading into the distance. More islands surfaced, punctuated with the tiny red-and-white cabins popular all over Scandinavia. Three hours into the journey, we were still floating past the archipelago's 28,000-plus landmasses.

My husband and I had caught a ride with Tallink's then 28-year-old *MS Regina Baltica* on a cloudy Friday afternoon. Despite her sturdiness and pretty makeup, she revealed her age through old industrial-style cabins and worn-out windows. Our captain switched effortlessly between Swedish, Latvian, and English over loud speakers as we entered open water.

Included in the ticket prices were two dinner buffets. I'd devised a food-ravishing plan that began with a massive salad. Then I approached the spread and it looked more like the seafood section at my grocery store. It was rich with mustard herring, onion herring, blackcurrant herring, Baltic herring rolls, hot-smoked herring, and cold-smoked herring. And that's before the roe and black caviar, followed by poached salmon, smoked salmon, salmon in shrimp sauce, etc. We stuffed ourselves on schools of fish rivaling those beneath the boat and then retired with 15 more hours to go.

Once in port, we discovered Riga's old town had cobblestone streets, open air cafés, and colorful historical buildings reminiscent of most old European cities'. Only signs in the *latviešu valoda* alphabet indicate that we're nowhere near France or Italy. We arrived on a moody day when the sun peeked teasingly from behind thick clouds. As we approached the castle, the stone-faced guards we'd noticed from a distance morphed into cute little teenagers flashing mischievous grins born from boredom, as they marched facing each other.

A short walk into old town and we arrived at a photography exhibition right in the heart of *Doma Laukums* (Dome Square). We spent the next half hour studying the array of people studying the exhibition. We filled up on history at the Museum of the Occupation of Latvia. Housed in a building resembling an above-ground bunker, its entrails were no laughing matter. The geographic reach of the Nazi regime was nothing short of unbelievable.

Riga was light on buskers. In fact, I spotted only two: A flutist in front of *Reformātu Baznīca* (Reformation Church) stopped after every second note in confusion and a lady well into her 60s — covered from head to toe in red plaid — exhibited her finest dancing moves: midair wrist-twists, followed by carefully executed spins, over and over again.

By the time we reached *Brīvības Piemineklis* (Freedom Monument), the sun was shining warmly, illuminating the city and making green spaces seem greener. A white limousine rolled up and gently poured out a beautiful bride and her prince. Then it also coughed up bridesmaids in corn-yellow dresses with turquoise sashes around their waists.

After hearty steaks at *Steiku Haoss*, we explored more of the city, including the *Vērmanes Dārzs* garden, and soaked up the beautiful spring weather along *Pilsētas Kanāls*, the metropolis's old moat. We soon discovered

the sun was being rationed. By late afternoon, heavy pelting rain sent us running back to the ship, as if spanking us for disembarking in the first place. Soaking wet, we finally boarded alongside cars and trucks being loaded into its belly.

Riga waved us off with the dark skies she'd welcomed us with. Then we faced that same buffet of herring and salmon on our way back. This time we dug into fruit-filled crepes for dessert, as harmonious voices sang traditional Swedish songs and hymns. They belonged to a choir on a weekend getaway. On other occasions, listening to those sweet sounds would have lifted my spirits. While cruising on open water amid the Baltic Sea, they were evocative of tragic final hours aboard the Titanic.

Pounding wind and the engine's slow hum reminded me we weren't dining on solid ground. Glancing out windows into pitch darkness, I realized the sea was more alive than the dark night belied and it filled me with a sense of awe. Our ship was but a speck on that deep expanse and we were at its mercy.

The next morning, we arrived back in Stockholm just hours before another cruise liner ran aground en route to Riga.

Dear Annikki

I didn't want her to see me like this.

When we met, I wore nothing but a damp towel. My hands were flapping to dry off silvery nail polish, its toxic acrylic scent already polluting the cramped hotel room.

She didn't care, shuffling from foot to foot, excitement oozing from every pore as she stepped into the room where my bridal party had convened to groom that morning.

"Ooooh! This is so exciting. Ooooh," she cooed in a heavy Finnish accent.

For years, I thought she had flaming red hair, remembering those faded sepia photographs my mom cherished so much. They spoke of worlds across oceans, funny customs, and heaps of snow. But here she was, strawberry blonde.

Age lines snaked across her face now, framing sparkling blue eyes that never had lost their youthful exuberance. She was tall and lean, in form-fitting jeans hugging a body that probably knocked socks off in its heyday.

"I'm so sorry you have to see me like this and..." I began an apology.

"I arrive from Helsinki. By boat," she interjected. "Viking Line. With my husband and son and... Ooooh!"

I would later find out they'd also flown from their little town in Northern Finland to board a ship in Helsinki and then sailed overnight to Stockholm for my wedding day.

The family had plans to head back the very next evening. However brief, their pilgrimage across the Baltic Sea needed to be made.

Studying this woman fidgeting in front of me, I still wasn't sure what had just transpired.

"Annikki?"

I pictured my mother as a 22-year-old nursing student in Nigeria's capital city at the time, Lagos. She's flipping through black-and-white newspapers, finally anchoring on a face. Mom probably thought it had brown eyes all those years.

I imagined her reading the accompanying words on a hot, humid African summer in 1975 and scribbling a neatly written letter to the address provided.

Advertisements for pen pals, they called them: pages upon pages filled with photographs and stories connecting Africans with fellow adventurous souls all across the globe. This cross-cultural pollination forged new friendships and broke down barriers back in the days when today's internet scammers were still being conceived and one could innocently advertise addresses in the national newspaper of a foreign country.

My mother's first words — in her fine calligraphic writing — would have gone like this: "Dear Annikki, my name is..." Then she would have waited patiently for weeks, hoping her writing charmed the woman behind the advert.

I imagined Annikki's first words back: "Dear Remi. Thank you for your wonderful letter..." Mom would have pored through that first note, studying the attached photograph — that sepia shot my family grew to know so well. In it, young Annikki wore a winter cap and coat. Mom probably thought that her new dark-eyed, red-haired Finnish friend lived where snow never ceased to fall.

That moment began a budding friendship only held back by oceans and miles. Each was the other's escape, the other's sounding board.

As the years passed, Annikki began to amass her own Polaroid archive from Nigeria. She probably had an image of me at just a few weeks old, bundled up in white lace like a Cabbage Patch doll, a stunned look on my chubby face brought on by the camera's otherworldly appearance and its unfamiliar flash. She'd have three more baby photographs once my siblings came along.

Dozens of carefully crafted letters had been mailed with international postage stamps. Elaborate birthday cards had been signed; stories of family, children, home, and country shared. As we grew older, we studied the joyful wedding photographs of her older sister.

We knew Annikki's name, like an aunt's.

Then time, the silent thief, would demand more of these correspondents. Time reprioritized their lives and they lost touch.

Five. Ten. Fifteen years.

Until that Google search five years ago in 2004.

I imagine my mother typing "A-N-N-I-K-K-I" with two index fingers, poking delicately at the keyboard, thin rimless glasses resting on the tip of her nose, hoping something — anything — would pop up.

And it would, with a hyphenated surname. Her Finnish friend had found love too. But without the hyphen, she might have stayed lost forever. That first email would have gone something like this: "Dear Annikki. Are you the same woman I shared some of my happiest moments with?"

"Ooooh! This is so exciting!" Annikki must have cooed

back, after confirming she was indeed the very same lady in the winter cap and coat from the faded image safely tucked away in a photo album.

They spent weeks, months, catching up on what time had stolen from their friendship. Letters replaced emails, printed photos bowed to digital attachments.

Then my mom called me.

"Guess whom I found? Guess whom I found!"

We invited her to the wedding and shuffled the seating chart once more. But this time, whining about changes would have been borderline blasphemy. How could I complain when fate had just orchestrated the perfect opportunity for an intercontinental friendship — formed years before my birth, over 40 years ago — to be finally consummated?

Annikki and my mother Remi met in the hotel lobby that morning.

I couldn't be there. After all, fake eyelashes still had to be applied and the bouquets of cream-and-yellow gerbera daisies tended to.

I heard their suffocating hug lasted three full minutes and was preceded by screams of joy. On first sight, their recognition had been instant, even though the dark-eyed, red-haired Finn had morphed into a strawberry-blond, blue-eyed woman in my mother's embrace.

I missed it. The mantilla veil was being clipped on and the last whiff of perfume applied. But I heard it was fantastic. Like a lover finally meeting a soul mate after 35 years of writing and baring all; touching and seeing each other for the very first time.

This moment was theirs, not mine.

Like an aunt, she sat right next to my parents on their proudest of days. She shimmied and swayed to traditional Nigerian beats, dancing into the wee hours of the morning.

Before she left, my mother and I vowed to make the same pilgrimage soon. Just like her family did, we would hop aboard the Viking Line and cruise overnight from Stockholm to Helsinki. We would then catch a flight and fly up north to the land where snow truly never ceases to fall.

Before time stole again.

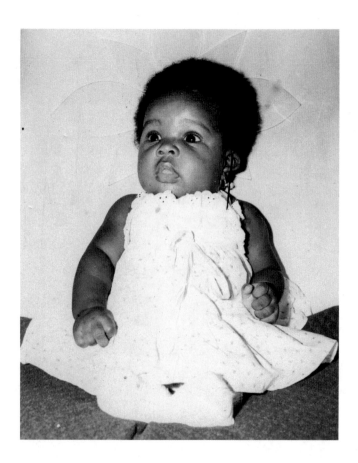

One Fine Swedish Day

The pungent smell of black coffee — followed by sweet wafts of spice — draws me out of bed and into the kitchen for breakfast. "Welcome to the wooorld!" my Swedish husband softly sings, while handing me a warm cinnamon bun. He slings his backpack over a shoulder and comes in for a quick kiss, before heading off to work at the newspaper.

I glance at our round kitchen clock and quickly scarf down the sugary bun. A 30-minute walk to the language school awaits me. Reaching for my own backpack, I stuff in scrap notes, two textbooks, and a dictionary the size of a small loaf of bread.

On the rickety elevator ride down past the apartment of Mr. Hussein from Iraq, I wonder when we were going to see him and his family, including his son Said, the pop singer. Once on the ground level, I poke my head into Tina's parlor for a quick hello. Soothing music and whiffs of massage balms meet me at the door. She greets me with a kiss, holds me at arm's length, and peers up through shiny eyes, dark like obsidian; each greeting reminiscent of long-lost friends reconnecting after decades. Except I'll see her again that same evening. She briefly tells me of her teenage son in Thailand and how he's been trying to get a visa for months.

"Don't forget your appointment," Tina yells after me in English tinged with a Thai accent. "We can always reschedule too," she adds. After all, she lives just one floor above me next to the Moldovans. I leave her with a smile and continue on, making my way past the modest five-table Japanese restaurant next door, remembering I still owe Suuni a sushi dinner order. *Unagi* (eel) sounds good, I think, strolling past the small neighborhood convenience store, where I occasionally get an onion or carton of milk on short notice while cooking.

"You should meet the two new attendants there," my husband shared not too long ago. "I think they're from Nigeria."

This morning, I see them — a young man and younger woman, running full speed to catch the train — and only manage a quick wave. I continue on my shortcut through sparse straggly woods, finally bursting onto a paved path. The trail takes me past the gym I sometimes visit, where young Iranian men lift weights and grunt so deeply that sometimes I flush, embarrassed.

The path winds past the Thai kiosk where Jen churns out scrumptious stir-fries and mouthwatering *pad prik king* (red curry with long beans). These meals lure me back so frequently that at our last meeting, she asked: "Are you pregnant?"

I carry on past the tan apartment block where Ricky from Serbia lives. In his early fifties, he physically

remains the envy of many in their thirties, including my husband who used to play basketball with him, along with Lukas from Greece. Now, time demands more from the trio, and their ball days seem a distant memory.

I notice Alganesh's petite form sauntering towards me, followed by a wide toothy smile and a tall unfamiliar man. "This is Bereket," she introduces after a quick "*hej*" (hi). "He's from Eritrea too!" Today, they join me on my walk, our destination the same. Our conversation ebbs and flows: from families left behind in homelands to new friends gained in foreign homes; from challenging pronunciations to differentiating between the sounds "*sjö*" and "*sju*" in Swedish words.

Eritrea. East Africa. I wonder if my friend Dayana from Colombia who works at the *resebyrå* (travel agency) might be running airfare specials to Kenya, Tanzania, and the spice isle of Zanzibar. I wonder if she has deals to Eritrea too. Then Alganesh and Bereket could see family more often.

Together we walk past a young shapely Muslim woman wearing a vivid blue Mona hijab over her head and shoulders, past the pizzeria run by bubbly Yüksel where I usually get juicy Turkish kebab pizzas on lazy evenings, past the basketball court where pubescent Swedish boys with sun-bleached blond hair shoot hoops.

Each neighborhood block seems like a jaunt across the globe.

We stumble into class seconds before our teacher Andy does. He sashays androgynously to the front of the spacious room. Raking delicate fingers through dyed blond hair, he welcomes us warmly. I'm not sure where he's from, but he speaks seven languages fluently including Swedish, which I am learning.

For those transitioning into a new country, there's that period, you know. The one wedged squarely between "mere traveler" and "bona fide local." Between a few basic phrases and true insider jokes. Immersion is the key to getting beneath a culture and fully learning its language, but what happens when you're not there yet? Especially when "there" seems to remain an ever-moving target?

As jumbled sentences slowly become recognizable and mumbled conversations drop a few understandable words, I notice other senses sharpening in the midst of it all.

Especially, observation.

I observe every single movement on my way to school — the waft of my husband's coffee, swaying vivid blues of hijabs headed to Swedish class, sweat running down fit bodies as they play basketball. I sit and observe as conversations grow heated and humorous in the local language.

I observe gestures. Eyes. Expressions. *Jaha! Vad kul! Just det!* (Oh! How cool! That's right!)

Observation becomes that intermediary that waits for language to grow. Once the words catch up, they merge with your observations and inch you even closer to being an authentic speaker.

That's where I am right now. I exist in a heightened sense of observation... or at least that's where I thought I was until I read some shocking news off my husband's iPhone on New Year's Eve. A famous Swedish actor had died in a house fire the very same day. Quickly turning to one of the other dinner guests, I tried explaining to her what I'd just read, expressing how horrendous it was.

She looked me straight in the eye for two seconds and burst out laughing.

I was confused. Why would someone's death generate

135

such forced laughter? She chuckled a bit more, nodded, and then turned away. We'd chatted freely earlier that evening — in Swedish — and the conversation had flowed both ways.

This time felt different and then I knew she hadn't understood a word, yet felt too polite to say she hadn't grasped it. If I'd been purely green, she might have stopped me or switched to English.

But she let me go on.

I'd finally moved into the class of language learners whose hands weren't being held anymore. I was in the sink-or-swim category; that nebulous transition period that feels like it lasts forever. I now call this the "plight of the intermediate speaker."

Moving through the beginning stages of Swedish was like hopping a cross-country flight from Los Angeles to New York. Sure, I encountered a few turbulent bumps along the way but it was a relatively smooth experience. I was then left standing on the shores of the Eastern U.S. about to swim across the intermediate Atlantic Ocean towards Scandinavia. My goal was to land on the fluent shores of Sweden before trekking upwards to Stockholm and finally mastering the language.

These are the four levels of language learning I've geographically mapped out for myself. Now I am mid-ocean, swimming hard as I can towards safety.

Sometimes, the waves carry me backwards. Other times, I surge past my fellow intermediates.

When another paddler pulls out an advanced word in class, I liken it to an unexpected swimming stroke. "That's new," I say to myself, as I push against the rogue waves of stagnancy.

Never one to overestimate my Swedish-speaking skills,

I know it's going to take some time to reach proper fluency. I may very well take a detour over to Greenland or Iceland and hang out there for awhile — plateaued in my speaking skills while mixing and matching words I already know to keep conversations going on deeper levels. And when I'm ready, I'll jump back in and continue my epic swim towards Sweden's shores and truly fluid communication. This means speaking without those awkward pauses to collect my thoughts and convert them from English.

Completing that final journey towards mastery remains my ultimate goal... and it could take decades. Right now, I need to keep treading water to stay afloat and just take it one stroke at a time.

And when I do get tired of treading, I'll use those sharpened observational skills as temporary arm-floats to stay alive.

The
Light Chasers

The narrow beam from my colleague Peter Rosén's headlamp illuminates the viewfinder on my camera, which is balanced atop his sturdy tripod. My own, a stable beast, seems flimsy that night as both dig into the calf-deep snow beneath us. He is pressing buttons with thinly gloved fingers, showing me controls, making sure I have the right settings. Or, rather, the perfect settings for capturing the only natural illumination: the Northern Lights. Green bands like folding curtains shimmer in the sky above and all around us. Peter's camera is already wirelessly at work, capturing a time-lapse of the gyrating Aurora Borealis, as he checks mine.

A staple on many travelers' bucket lists, these unpredictable phenomena occur when solar explosions cause particles from the sun to collide with gases in the earth's atmosphere, creating vibrant red, green, and sometimes fuchsia bands of light. While NASA dutifully monitors the sun's flares, catching a glimpse of the Northern Lights is never guaranteed. Even throwing in ideal weather conditions — crispy, cold, clear, cloudless skies with little to no moonlight — promises you nothing.

An aurora photographer, Peter moved to northern Sweden's Abisko 14 years ago and has been shooting the lights ever since. He and his colleagues follow NASA's monitoring website like scripture. They know the strongest displays appear 24 to 48 hours after a solar explosion. Their gear boxes are always packed and ready with two to three tripods and cameras, several wide-angle lenses furiously cleaned each night to remove frost and dust spots, and enough battery life to beat the threatening cold. They've captured thousands of images and seem to have seen it all.

Yet Peter is out here in a borderline reverent state, making sure my settings are absolutely perfect because those lights deserve nothing short of perfection. Then he

139

turns to the sky, observing and soaking up the display, his own camera forgotten in the background.

Even though he knew about the solar explosions and the possibility of the lights showing up sometime tonight based on NASA predictions, we were outside by exactly 9pm, scanning the sky because of Sámi elder Anders Kärrstedt's advice.

A few minutes earlier, Anders had stepped out into that dark February night and had begun watching the horizon. He manages the reindeer lodge Nutti Sámi Siida alongside Nils Nutti and his family members. Together they welcome travelers to experience elements of their indigenous Sámi lifestyle, from corralling reindeer at

the lodge to cooking *souvas* (smoked reindeer meat) over open flames, skimming through winter landscapes on reindeer sleds and scanning for the Aurora Borealis while sitting out in a Nordic tipi.

Anders studied the shapes of the clouds and the direction of the wind. Very little activity. A mild green line fizzed here and there.

He looked down at his watch. The lights should appear within the next two hours, he told me. And like clockwork, they begin glowing a few minutes past 9pm and then they burst into vibrant greens, purples, and pinks, canvasing the entire sky and leaving me at a loss for words.

Peter and I grab our cameras and tripods, and trot into the darkness, hoping the lights will dance long enough for us to set up our gear.

Of course Anders takes no credit. "When it comes to me making predictions, it is pure luck," he shares. "From experience, you know approximately when to expect Northern Lights, but there's no science around it. It's more like you get a feeling for when it might occur, but many times you are not even close."

This gut feeling intrigues me. I want to know just how deeply the Sámi culture intertwines with nature and if — or what — its people could predict regarding the auroras.

Roughly 70,000 Sámi live in Norway, Sweden, Finland, and the Russian Kola Peninsula: an area collectively known as the "Sápmi region." Approximately 20,000 of them dwell in Swedish Lapland. For centuries — arguably thousands of years — they have taken their cues from the wilderness.

I got more insight into this intricate relationship while riding alongside Nils through the snow- and ice-coated Arctic tundra en route to the town of Abisko in Swedish Lapland. Northern Lights mythology remains very important to the Sámi because, according to their religion, life first descended to earth through the aurora, he tells me. "The white big male reindeer is holy because it came from the sky riding on the dancing aurora," he shares, his eyes never leaving the narrow asphalt road ahead, which cuts through the pristine, white, eerily silent landscape as we forge towards Abisko.

The same way Anders observes patterns in the sky and anticipates its curtains of color, Nils often looks to the Northern Lights to forecast the next day's weather, especially when he is somewhere remote with his herd of reindeer. Because the Sámi were nomadic for centuries, they learned the weather's moods and how to prevent dangerous risks when heading into the tundra or mountains.

"For example, we can see in the Northern Lights if strong hard winds are coming tomorrow. If they dance a lot across the sky with lots of shifting patterns, we know that strong winds are coming tomorrow," Nils shares. "If it's a cloudy green aurora, then you know it's going to be relatively stable weather tomorrow."

The Sámi have a close relationship with the lights but they don't seem to be "chasers" like Peter on quests for the perfect shots. I want to get behind the psyche of those who hunted the aurora for a living. What moved these poetic souls who never tired of those green and red swirls unfolding across the sky, despite thousands of similar photos already in their archives?

Nils, Peter, and I are heading to Abisko because the region has been scientifically proven to be Sweden's most ideal viewing spot, due to a unique microclimate. Abisko National Park lies 43 miles (70km) along Lake Torneträsk, which helps create the famous "blue hole" — a patch of sky that remains clear regardless of the surrounding weather patterns.

Just 48 hours after a solar explosion, the strongest lights are coming and Abisko is the place to be. Peter offers photo courses for tourists during the peak viewing season — December to early April — in the park and at the Aurora Sky Station, an observation center atop Mount Nuolja. "The landscape, wildlife, and everything that belongs to the wilderness of Lapland inspires me to find new photographic projects and it surprises me quite often that I can get so excited about new aurora displays although I have seen thousands of them during my 14 years," Peter shares with me. "I love photographing light," he goes on to say, "and the dancing queen of the northern sky is certainly the most spectacular of them all. Every evening is different and when it comes to photographing, there is always something new to explore and improve."

Another Abisko-based photographer, Chad Blakley, has been running workshops for five years and has also dedicated his career to the Northern Lights. "I hold the opinion that there is no natural display of beauty that can compete with the magic and splendor of the Aurora Borealis," Chad notes. "There really is no better sight than a powerful aurora dancing over your head."

Every photographer I talk to echoes similar sentiments. The unpredictability keeps them coming back out every night, scanning for a blaze of glory even in frigid temperatures. I reached out to Astrophotographer Göran Strand, who has been chasing the Northern Lights since 2003. "I've been interested in astronomy ever since childhood, so being out under a starry night is something I've done my entire life," he says. "Every light is unique in shape, color, and strength, so you never know what to expect when going out to watch it. The most intriguing thing I've learned, after all these years, is that the Northern Lights still amaze me."

All these light-hunters were on to something. The mystical shape-shifting auroras morph and transform; no two events are ever the same or even remotely close. This keeps up the intrigue. Like couples who've been married for years and fan their passion by being unpredictable, this dance between the Northern Lights and her dedicated cadre of photographers is strangely romantic.

Dare I say it? The light chasers may very well have fallen for the Aurora Borealis. After all, only true love can lure one to camp for hours every night in pitch-dark subzero temperatures...

I remember the first time I saw those swirling green and red lights rippling across the winter sky. It was in Reykjavík in 2006. I squealed like a kid and grabbed onto a fellow traveler. And then I fell silent and just looked, completely absorbed in the seducing swirl.

There's something about the Northern Lights dance that forces you to pause. You ignore your camera perched atop its sturdy tripod. You put your smartphone away and just watch, totally engrossed.

Bewitched, entranced, and in awe, you exist fully in the moment, acutely aware of your breathing and pounding heart. You realize just how small you are in the grand scheme of life as the sky gyrates.

Viewing the lights might elicit a slow whistle of appreciation. But I know better. Like attractive women sashaying down sidewalks or shirtless well-cut construction workers, they are meant to be respected and catcalls can sit poorly. Anders agrees: "You're not allowed to whistle at the lights because you may annoy it and that's dangerous. You can be burned."

And no one ever wants to get burned in a relationship.

Decoding
Lagom

Eight of us — six Swedes, one Finn, and me — are gathered in a modest, city-center studio apartment in Stockholm's eclectic Södermalm district. Next to our dinner table is a small window with a gorgeous view of the history-rich old town, Gamla Stan, with its narrow fingerlike melon, red clay, and burnt sienna structures. The location alone makes this apartment as coveted as a New York City penthouse with direct views of the Empire State Building.

My friend Jörgen is making single cups of coffee on a mini French press as we each wait silently in turn. The quiet leaves me unsettled, almost feeling obliged to fill it with random chitchat, a few words about the weather. I glance from silent guest to silent guest. Surely I can't be the only one struck by this stillness? When Jörgen hands over a coffee, talk resumes again as if trying not to exclude him from any of our conversations.

Then we fall mute as he presses the next cup.

I had noticed this pattern before. Once at Stockholm's Arlanda airport, after flying in from Swedish Lapland, we passengers waited in utmost quiet for about 30 minutes for our delayed luggage.

Back home in the U.S., I'd have nudged the nearest fellow, hissed, and shook my head. Then we would have commiserated in loud booming voices about this baggage delay.

Here stating the obvious seems unnecessary. So instead of filling the emptiness, we wait patiently until everyone has their coffee before easing back into camaraderie. There is a certain air of self-assuredness among this table of well-travelled, world-class musicians from the Royal Philharmonic Orchestra that I am dining with, but no-one shares any personal achievements until asked. They don't talk over each other either. Everyone speaks three or four languages fluently but dismisses their skill because they are not native speakers. Dressed in worn-out jeans, single-color shirts or blouses, and sock-clad feet, they could not look more ordinary.

I'd long heard of this unspoken custom before moving to Sweden a couple years ago. This untranslatable ethos called "*lagom*" (pronounced "law-gum") permeates all facets of the Swedish psyche: its culture, lifestyle, business, and society. Often misconstrued as indifference or the stereotypical Scandinavian "coldness," *lagom* is loosely translated from Swedish as "appropriate, in moderation or just the right amount." For example, you could say "the bath is *lagom* hot" or "the coffee is *lagom* strong."

Speaking of coffee, *mellanbrygg* (medium brew) dominates the store shelves. Many Swedes have a hard time deciding between light and strong blends so they gravitate towards the middle, the medium, the *lagom* brew. This same risk-aversive logic also applies to milk: *mellanmjölk* (medium milk) remains the popular choice, causing Swedes to give their country the moniker "land of *mellanmjölk*."

For me, *lagom* harkens back to British Author Robert Southey's 1837 fairy tale *Goldilocks and the Three Bears* where his blonde lead character sat in the chair, slept in the bed, and ate the porridge that felt "just right." No need for excess, bragging, exaggerations, unnecessary public displays, or showiness... Far from

denoting complacency, the idea carries with it an air of appropriateness. And it makes sense in a socialist state, which promotes equality and moderation on all levels. An excellent Swedish review after a fantastic meal could be *"det var inget fel på det här"* (there was nothing wrong with this).

Not-so-team-like demise

The word *"lagom"* itself comes from a shortening of the phrase *"laget om,"* which literally means "around the team" and dates back to the Viking era between the 8th and 11th centuries. Communal horns filled with *mjöd* (mead) were often passed around and everyone sipped only their share.

I imagine any Viking who took a quick extra gulp met with some not-so-team-like demise. These fierce warriors would later sail on and pillage across Europe, Asia, and today's bastion of capitalism North America, each acquiring their own individual horn to gulp from, I would assume.

Ironically, while today's Sweden is known for its fresh cutting-edge designs, futuristic ways of thinking, and fierce modernism, this unspoken way of conduct and living is deep-seated in campfire traditions from the past.

Booming braggart in the room

"I love *lagom!*" says Linda Henriksson, a teacher and native Swede. "It's so individual. It could mean anything to anyone. Ironically, "average" could be many different things depending on whom you're talking to." So the word itself was now being used in everyday settings to mean "just right." And "just right" for you could be different from what's "just right" for me. So a *lagom*-paced jog for Linda might be a run, considering

146

her long lean frame, while I would veer towards a leisurely stroll.

According to the government agency Statistiska Centralbyrån, over 9.5 million people call Sweden home. Nearly one in five residents has a foreign background, bringing in differing cultural beliefs and traditions, which might be slowly diluting this intrinsic Swedish concept.

On the contrary, Linda thinks non-native Swedes are adopting this norm pretty quickly. Many consider *lagom* funny at first, because it is untranslatable. But once you realize you're the only booming braggart in the room a couple times, you might start looking deeper into cultural nuances. In essence, "feeling out the social code within the group you're hanging with," she explains.

I come from two boisterously competitive cultures — Nigerian and American — where everyone grows talons and claws their way to survive, stand out, and succeed. The word "*lagom*" felt almost blasphemous at first. Yet I embraced it like a lunch buffet after a 30-day Sahara Desert crossing. To me, it meant the cool restraint of self-confidence. A poise that meant I didn't need to boast or brag about my achievements, but actually let my work do the talking for me.

World-class egos

I reach out to my friend Fredrik Rydehäll, a lighting engineer working where big egos come out to play — in the performing arts. His job is to literally put the actor, singer, or dancer in the spotlight. He has seen a broad range of personalities — from the grandstanding choreographer behind the scenes to the outstanding-yet-humble ballerina on stage. "It is easier to stand out in Stockholm because it's so multicultural and very diverse," Fredrik says. He's from relatively tiny Luleå and "in smaller towns, it's harder to stand out because there's a lot less diversity," he adds.

147

I ponder his logic. So in essence, Swedes could get away with not being so *lagom* in a bigger city while lost in the crowd.

But then nuances enter into the mix. "It really depends on why you want to stand out," Fredrik continues. "If you stand out because you are that way, then it's good. If you stand out because you just want to get attention, then it's annoying."He points out an over-the-top Swedish personality with a deep orange suntan, whom we both know. "He's playing a role and that's really ridiculous. He's trying to stand out because he likes to stand out, not because he's really like that as a person."

I also track down Mats Olsson in Ukraine. This well-known sports columnist for the daily newspaper *Expressen* was covering the European Championship football games in Kiev. Sweden had just been kicked out of its group pool amidst high expectations, and the collective mood in Stockholm was "oh well, next time,"

paired with shoulder shrugs of disappointment. Had Sweden played horrendously, I would have understood the shrugs, but the team had worked really hard together. I was expecting a national outcry.

Even on such a global stage, it seems Swedish teams have been conditioned to temper their feelings, to be not too heated and not too lackadaisical either. According to Mats, two high-profile Swedes who personify *lagom* while displaying world-class talent are ice hockey legend Peter Forsberg and soccer star Henrik Larsson, both now retired. "After amazing performances, their replies during interviews were mostly along the lines of 'well, I guess it was okay, it was the team that won.' Or 'if I was good, it's for others to judge, I do my job for the team,' and 'as long as we win the games, it doesn't matter who scores,'" he notes. Their humility may be lagom; their athletic prowess and mindsets were anything but. Even celebrating feats of success had to be done in moderation, it turns out.

148

Quick right
at Sven's red cottage

In all its inexplicable mystery, the core virtue of *lagom* greatly appeals to me and magnifies as I spend more time in Northern Sweden and Swedish Lapland. There long winter nights force you into the arms of your neighbors and friends to survive mentally and physically, fostering tightly knit relationships and kinships in the tiniest of villages.

At the height of those infamous, bitingly cold Scandinavian winters, only an hour of daylight helps to maintain one's sanity in places deep within the Arctic Circle like Kiruna, the country's northernmost town. Even the frozen tundra models itself after *lagom* as you drive along the E4 highway gradually making your way towards the map's edge. Tall pine trees sparsely punctuate the terse terrain, as if questioning why thick branch-to-branch forests are needed. Classic *stugor* (cottages) add bursts of brick-red color.

This deep, coppery shade — Falu red — is named after the village Falun in Dalarna, where it originated. Between the 16th and 19th centuries, this paint was the cheapest available and so many cottages had that same rich, cozy hue. If you had a bit more funds, you could paint your cottage yellow or white. But that was about the extent of showiness allowed.

I wonder how people gave each other directions before the invention of road signs. "Go down the road until you see Nilsson's red cottage, then turn left and keep straight until Arvid's red cottage comes into view. Take a quick right at Sven's red cottage before you finally arrive at Olof's red cottage."

As you press northwards, the UNESCO World Heritage Site Gammelstad Church Town drives homes this point of standing in line and not sticking out. It has 400-plus *stugor* built wall-to-wall in a circular fashion around the 15th-century stone-walled Nederluleå Kyrka (church).

Fair maidens
in flowing summer frocks

I find winter to be hands down the best season to visit Sweden. True, summer evokes visions of fair maidens in flowing frocks with garlands of wild flowers woven through long blonde locks, all swirling around a maypole. But one fully appreciates the rugged side of Sweden during its darkest months.

That rugged side trudges through silky white snow on skis, in snowshoes, atop a snowmobile, or on a sled drawn by Siberian Huskies in subzero temperatures. It roasts *korv* (sausages) over open flames, while the Aurora Borealis shimmers across the clear, cool night sky. It cross-country skies along the Kebnekaise mountains and the foothills of Mount Kebne in Swedish Lapland, or along Kungsleden (King's Trail) located 125 miles (200km) inside the Arctic Circle.

At least that's what the son of my mother-in-law's neighbor did solo for two months... just for the fun of it.

No gallant screams of victory

Tiny tire spikes crunch through compact snow — the only sound for miles, other than the racing engine that my in-law Mikael is driving at seemingly insane speeds. Fresh, knee-deep snow cakes the landscape. His archaic Ford has a manual gear shift that is only a metal rod sticking out between the front seats. The steering wheel is also bare metal. Fixed atop the car are giant headlamps to pierce the pitch-black "night" that will fall in the early afternoon.

"You'll be fine," he assures me, seconds before a potentially harrowing head-on collision with a snowmobile that appears out of nowhere. Then he drives across a frozen lake to meet up with eight other guys waiting for the rally. Hands in pockets, they stand silently, their faces as ice cold as our surroundings. Short *"hej's"* (hellos) and quick nods are exchanged. Each has a makeshift race car — banged-up Volvos, beaten-down Saabs, and, of course, our battered Ford.

We wait in silence for others to arrive. There are no jeers or taunting like you might expect at a race. We stand frozen against the landscape like ice sculptures.

This makeshift village contest is a way to pass time during the frigid days. It's a tradition shared from grandparents to grandsons and granddaughters: racing across the frozen lake in oval laps carved through the snow, as a way of keeping busy and beating the winter blues.

Soon enough, our little rally begins and cars race at breakneck speeds, sliding across ice and rounding sharp corners. One wrong move and they'd cartwheel into the trees. Still no screams of joy or excitement echo... Only even-keeled laughs when vehicles spin out of control and need to be dug out.

"Your turn." I pretend not to hear, but there is no avoiding it. I climb into the passenger seat and fumble nervously with my seatbelt. I grab onto the bar above my window for support and say a silent prayer. My quiet lasts only until Mikael hits the accelerator, but my belly-wrenching screams of sheer terror are met only with a quiet laugh as we speed around at up to 60mph (100km/hour). On pure ice, it feels like twice that. We slide sideways at sharp bends, and tauntingly bump one of the Volvos.

Our rally continues until the sun sets at 2pm, but I can't distinguish the victors from the losers. No extravagant displays of emotions unfold. No screams of victory. The thrill is to be experienced only behind the wheel and not expressed outwardly.

Lagom's ugly cousin — *jante*

If *lagom* is a humble considerate gentleman, the fictitious *jantelagen* (law of Jante) is his uglier, more cynical cousin that pretty much states "don't think you're anyone special or that you're better than us!"

To the untrained eye in casual Swedish settings, you might not know which norm — *lagom* or *jante* — is at play.

"A lot of Swedes hate *lagom* too," my friend Linda explains. "Mostly because of the *jantelagen* aspect. Maybe you as a Swede want to be noticed, but you feel you can't scream as loud as you'd want to because you can't be too much or too little of anything."

Conceptualized in a novel by Danish-Norwegian author Aksel Sandemose in 1933, the Law of Jante not only frowns upon individual success and achievements, but also discourages individuality in favor of collective unity.

Beneath this group mentality breeds deep-seated jealousy prevalent within the culture and directed towards successful Swedes. All without being verbalized, of course.

My Swedish husband Urban weighs in: "Swedes talk about '*den svenska avundsjukan*' (the Swedish jealousy)." This is not to be confused with regular jealousy, which might motivate someone to action. Instead this icy northern envy seethes silently into the grave, while maintaining its personal status quo.

And thanks to *jante* adding an unattractive complex layer atop *lagom*, many of the country's critics feel this mentality promotes dependence on social welfare, stifles ambition, and is non-confrontational, hence why Sweden stayed neutral in many world conflicts and wars.

Ditching *lagom* into the Baltic Sea

Once a norm I thought intrinsic and immutable, it seems *lagom* can be slunk into and stripped off like lingerie when necessary. When many Swedes cross international borders, they figuratively scream at the top of their lungs, wear their patriotism like tattoos, and let loose away from their home shores... only to fall back in line — or "queue," as it were — when they return.

Overnight Baltic cruises remain an outlet for Swedes to lose *lagom*. Boats depart from Stockholm's harbor on Friday afternoons, sailing the Baltic Sea overnight. They arrive in Latvia by daybreak and passengers can spend Saturday exploring Riga at a breakneck speed before catching a ride home, landing on Sunday morning. These short getaways also hit Tallinn, Helsinki, Saint Petersburg, and a handful of other Baltic ports. A roundtrip fare is often cheaper than dinner at an average Stockholm restaurant.

I gave it a try on the *MS Galaxy* — a popular overnight ferry to Turku, Finland. Girls in their early twenties huddled on a metal bench in the boarding hall. They seemed like mannequins, hidden beneath layers of pale matte foundation, multiple coats of rose blush, and smoky black eye-shadow that made already piercing blue eyes like glacial shards. Skinny legs clad in black patchy pantyhose were crossed, their top limbs rocking in unison. Dozens of them — maybe hundreds — sat on low benches, leaned against walls, and stood in circles. Some giggled, others fidgeted nervously.

Behind me milled hundreds of boys, often holding half-drunk Carlsberg beers. I saw two dominant styles: gelled, sleeked-back dark hair and short, spiky blond hair. Like the security guard who was walking his sniffing German Shepherd through the crowd, the boys were surveying the room — tagging and marking — before boarding.

On the *Galaxy*, they'll make their moves. Now wasn't the time to walk up to the skittish fillies. And so the boys stood with their chests puffed out, cradling beer cans, chatting while scanning the girls with laser-like precision.

My husband and I were caught amidst their flirtatious crossfire. Initially hoping for a relaxing weekend away from Stockholm, we were beginning to have a slight hunch we'd picked the wrong cruise. People kept their distance, yet I could sense the weight of anticipation, mixed with that remarkable sense of restraint. This shape-shifting unspoken restraint I'd now embraced since moving to Sweden from its capitalist cousin, the United States.

Our destination was Finland... well, the seaport of Turku, but only long enough to unload and onboard passengers. We were barely scraping the country. Once we set sail, the ruckus onboard rivaled a fraternity party and the noisy revels continued all night. In fact, I arrived at the breakfast buffet just minutes after a naked Swede has strolled through.

Floating on international waters, away from home and those unspoken rules that govern society, Swedes gladly chuck *lagom* overboard, only to fish it back up before docking in Stockholm.

The Crayfish Experience

Out in the lush green backyard, old wooden tables are strewn together and covered with white linen, well-worn from use. Cozy wool blankets, some frayed with age, line benches. White paper napkins top glass plates from various collections.

The warm glow from lanterns and candles flickers against red wine bottles, little clusters of mini whiskies, and carafes of sparkling water. Loaves of freshly baked walnut-, olive- and tomato-bread lie next to blocks of moldy cheeses on wooden serving slabs. For sides, a pasta and pea salad joins the quiche made with sundried tomatoes, spinach, and olives.

Next to plates are photocopied sheets of old Swedish drinking songs — just to start us off. Soon we'll all be belting out the classics together.

Friends — old and new — dig into bowls of crayfish, hungrily cracking red shells. We pull at tender orangish pieces of flesh while sucking salty juice from the shells.

A few drops of rain arrive. Within minutes, a makeshift tarp is made from boat sails tied to trees and propped up with wooden sticks.

We revel in this ritual of a warm August evening crayfish party, simple and unpretentious.

FINAL THOUGHTS

Brown-Eyed Girl
Meets Blue-Eyed Boy

What would I say to my 12-year-old self, if I could return to the village of Badore along the Lekki Peninsula's shores, circa the early 90s? What would I reveal to that girl, balancing a metal bucket full of water on low-cropped hair?

Probably nothing, to be honest.

I'd observe her carrying that heavy burden, steadying it with one hand while the other smooths her gingham uniform with its brown-and-white checkered pattern. Her rubber sandals kick small pebbles down the dusty road, which leads back to her boarding school dormitory.

Speechless, I'd just look, unwilling to interrupt this familiar routine of hers. I'd be too scared to explain that her future children would have a different mother tongue. My preteen self is too young to process it all, to understand the trajectory her life will take. It will catapult her across various continents, challenging her to face a world much larger than her young mind comprehends.

I'd watch her go, wobbling to adjust as the bucket swings sharply. That container of cold water — drawn from the village well — will last her until the next day. It's enough for a bath, brushing her teeth, and other menial tasks, because the faucets have been nonfunctional for months. Once by her bunk bed, she carefully lifts the bucket off her head with outstretched arms straining under its weight. Quickly pouring in a capful of the antiseptic Dettol to kill bacteria, she pushes the bucket under her bed for safe storage, yanks aside her mosquito net, and climbs underneath to rest for awhile before the school bell rings for dinner. Except she's not resting; I can tell from her eyes, which look straight up at the bunk above her. She seems deep in thought and I wish I could crawl into her mind, into her subconscious, to let her know that her future isn't what she fears. She half-cocks her head, as if someone is whispering into her ear. Her eyebrows arch in worry.

I think she senses my presence.

Meanwhile, thousands of miles away, less than two hours south of the Arctic Circle, an 18-year-actor stands on stage at the local theater in Luleå. He wears navy blue overalls and a striped train conductor's cap. Tall and straggly, he rocks on his heels as he spews lines of Swedish. He makes a funny face and the crowd of about 100 roars with laughter. This modest act goes on for an hour more before the actors gather and take their bows. The young man takes another quick bow, waves to the crowd, and jogs backstage. In the makeshift dressing room, he sits, shoulders leaning back, staring at his reflection in the narrow mirror. Unsuspecting blue eyes stare back at him. He sighs in frustration. All this is beginning to get to him. This small town, this place, this scene — it's all too familiar, too comfortable. There is something more out there.

Fika, that ritual of coffee and pastries, unfolds yet again. He'd grown up on its distinct smell: that strong spicy blast of freshly brewed java, that sweet sugary waft of freshly baked *kanelbullar* (cinnamon buns). He reaches for one, stares at its familiar roundness, and takes a large bite.

———

If you'd told me years ago — while I was growing up in the bustling city of Lagos, Nigeria — that my babies' first language would be Swedish, I probably would have laughed. Or, better yet, I might have completely ignored you, because how could such a thing happen to me? What on earth would tie me to such a foreign land, an unfamiliar world in so many ways?

Race was never an issue for me growing up in Nigeria. Everyone was just as black as me. The Igbo were yellower in their blackness, the Hausa were ashier in their blackness, and the Yoruba — my tribe — were chocolaty in their blackness. Yet we were all the same. Sweden meant absolutely nothing to me.

Even with my knowledge of geography, I still couldn't point it out on a map at that time. I just knew it was somewhere in Europe and that it wasn't Switzerland. ABBA had infiltrated my home through the LPs we danced to at birthday parties, yet I didn't find out the group was Swedish until decades later. I'd snipped out a picture of actor Dolph Lundgren from a magazine and pasted it on the cover of a fiction series that written as a teenager. But I never knew his nationality. And while Nigeria's national football team always seemed to end up in the same World Cup pool as Sweden, that country still meant nothing to me.

Looking back now, it seemed Sweden had somehow started seeping into my subconscious in various ways, but I just never made any concrete connections to it.

My path northwards began once I moved to the States, starting college at 15. There my ethnicity was highlighted, magnified, and thrown right in my face. I'd never been more fully aware of being African than I was while carving my way as a teenager through America's divided society.

Even more unsettling was having someone else's history and struggles pushed upon my teenage psyche, and I refused to quietly slide into society's preset box for me. If I didn't do that in my own country of Nigeria, why would I start now in someone else's — the U.S.?

To break away from local stereotypes and expectations of me as a black woman in the '90s, I just did what I naturally liked. These things happened to be unconventional from what blacks in America were "supposed" to enjoy. I played rugby, traveled abroad frequently, tried adventure racing and listened to emo

music (I hated hip-hop). I dated whom I liked regardless of race, even venturing onto matchmaking sites before they were popular.

It was that simple.

As a person who has always followed her heart, my marriage couldn't be more conventional to me. Still, I understand why people feel our relationship lies out of the norm. Not only are we an interracial, intercultural couple, but we also met online back in 2006, when critics thought finding love via the internet reeked of desperation. For me, it made the most sense as a traveler. I was always on the road for work and for pleasure, roving freely from Africa and North America to Asia, Europe, and the South Pacific.

Being on the move meant not having time to really invest in serious relationships back home. If anything, getting into something steady required me sitting tight for awhile and running across potential partners in church, parks, or grocery stores in more conventional ways like I was supposed to.

The internet let me weed out time wasters, though. Then I met my future husband online. Daily calls and Skype sessions gave us that chance to get to know each other as friends before meeting in person a few months later.

I'll always remember his first email message to me — the very first contact. Right there and then, he already knew the odds were stacked against us, even beyond the distance, spanning the entire Atlantic Ocean. "I know we'll probably never meet up for coffee," his email started. "But I just wanted to let you know that you seem like a really special person and I think we have a lot in common."

Seriously?

This I had to hear because on paper we weren't supposed to work. I come from one of West Africa's more boisterous tribes — the Yoruba. We punctuate every sentence with a dramatic "ah" for effect. We talk loudly while flailing our arms in explanation and point to nearby objects using pursed lips, not fingers.

Urban hails from northern Sweden, a region whose inhabitants are not known for voluble small talk. These people inhale sharply to let you know they're quietly following your chatter, hands firmly tucked in their pockets.

I pondered what on earth we'd have in common.

I imagined him peeling the tin cover off a can of herring and pouring bite-sized pieces of fish onto a plate already loaded with yellow almond potatoes. Meanwhile, back home in Nigeria, we would be readying a pot of boiling hot water for the freshly killed chicken whose feathers we were about to pluck.

We were strangers in every sense of the word, living parallel lives that neither of us suspected would one day intersect in such a profound way.

Still, I responded out of curiosity.

Thus I uncovered the first of many things we would have in common: he was a journalist. A writer. He knew how to string words together that kept me engaged and coming back for more. His emails were called "reports" and he painted pictures of his surroundings and what he was doing. His missives started out like Swedish noir novels, and I kept on reading.

Two weeks later, I heard his voice for the first time. I already knew so much about him by then. We talked for hours, painting pictures of how we did absolutely nothing that day or that evening. We would uncover so many more values we had in common — from a deep faith in God, which guided our daily decisions, to our profound love of exploring new cultures, languages, and destinations. Over the next five months, we became fast friends who confided in each other. When we finally met that summer in Stockholm, his first words to me were "hello, stranger!"

Shortly after that first trip, he came over to the U.S.

during my sister Dami's wedding. I remember the first time he walked into our home; the first time he met my parents. My dad observed him quietly with eyes peering over rectangular-shaped glasses as Urban's tall frame roamed around our home.

I could clearly read my dad's thoughts. "Who on earth has Lola dragged home?"

That first winter together, my new boyfriend took me up to Swedish Lapland, to the ice-coated world he grew up in. One where I would learn to ride a snowmobile and go joyriding on a frozen lake, tucked into layers upon layers of warm clothing, trying to moderate my breath in double-digit subzero temperatures. Where

wild moose and reindeer darted across the narrow streets and hotels were built from ice; where seeing the elusive Northern Lights was like watching the sun rise every day. His family and life seemed so normal to him, yet wildly exotic to me. I saw in person all that he'd described to me, and I began to understand his wanderlust for something more.

Distance messes with you. It plays mental games, which can make you question if you'd imagined the relationship in the first place. Maybe I'd simply dreamed up this beguiling man on another continent? As doubt began to creep in, after a few weeks apart, we two strangers

would make the journey once more — battling the airport lines and uncomfortable questions about the "purpose of the visit" at passport control. We would reconnect and find our center together.

Even my corporate bosses noticed it.

They caught my blank stares at meetings and realized my decade-long programming career was no longer my first passion. Sooner or later, something had to give, but I was working on a few key projects that I just couldn't walk away from. My work was already partly location-independent, and after a few weeks of convincing, my bosses allowed me to work remotely. Today I credit this generous act for keeping our budding relationship on track.

Over the next three years, we would spend significant chunks of time frequently traversing three distinct worlds — Sweden, the U.S., and Nigeria. I remember his very first trip to my native country.

My true home.

──────────

"There's no way she's going to get it in." He was confident. We were sitting on the tarmac aboard our KLM flight in Amsterdam. Both of us, along with a newly befriended seatmate, were wagering as a middle-aged Nigerian woman kept shoving bulky square luggage into the shallow rectangular overhead bin.

"Trust me, it will enter," our new lady pal from Benin was certain.

"Absolutely no way... No? What?" Much like a magic trick, the baggage had miraculously fit. I beamed at her triumph. Disbelief washed over Urban and I knew he was in for quite the ride once he got to Nigeria. After landing, seat belts snapped open before we'd even

taxied off the runway. As we rolled past airline carcasses of the now-defunct Nigerian Airways, I glanced over to observe his disposition.

Lagos assaults all five senses: unprepared visitors are usually left shaken and in shock. The sheer volume of people per square foot instantly overwhelms. Over 150 million residents live in Nigeria, an area roughly the size of Texas. Between 15 to 23 million of those are rumored to dwell in Lagos, easily a couple million too many. Sweden has a little over nine million total.

In the three hours it took us to travel roughly 37 miles (60km) home from the airport, we'd seen at least a million people, including toddlers, dart through traffic as drivers honked impatiently. And the okadas (motorcycle taxis) — or "mosquitoes" as my dad calls them — whizzed between cars, thumping on our car trunk or hood if we didn't let them squeeze through.

"There's so much chaos," Urban noted. "But somehow it works. It just seems to work and I don't get it!"

That first trip of his — a quick 10-day jaunt for family celebrations — saw us traversing the megacity of Lagos and neighboring states. I also introduced him to authentic Yoruba culture and cuisine along the way. It was exhausting.

But from hand-sized black snails to roasted goat meat, he downed it all with Viking valor. A quick trip to the tailor, and three days later he was modeling his own custom-made traditional ankara outfits. After a couple electrical outages, he was yelling at the power company alongside the rest of us. Booming and excitable voices became the norm and his pitch grew louder.

Within days, he'd begun to morph into one of thousands of expatriates that just can't seem to leave Nigeria behind and, frankly, don't want to.

"What are you doing?" I found him scribbling away on a small piece of paper one lazy afternoon.

"Oooh, just compiling an A to Z of Lagos... 'G' for goat meat... 'H' for humidity... 'S' for serious faces... 'T' for traffic jams..."

Lagos had charmed him like I knew she would, and as he wrote away in full concentration, deep down I knew I'd found him. The "him" that I'd prayed for, for so many years; the "him" whose qualities and virtues I'd written down in a bulleted list like so many other single women looking for love.

We were married a year later.

———

I sit, gently stroking my pregnant bulge. I'm sometimes excited, sometimes anxious, and oftentimes, confused. This child growing within me has two cultures, which couldn't be more different and have absolutely nothing to do with each other. Yet they'll be forever intertwined for this new soul inside me.

My husband walks in with coffee and a plate of *kanelbullar*. Earlier that day, I'd sent him on a quest around town in search of goat meat. He kept texting photos from his smartphone of each cutlet he found. "Is this it? No? What about this?"

I reach for a warm bun, studying it. "Would you like me to bake these for you one day?" I ask, turning to observe his face as well. His eyes light up and a small grin frames his face.

"That would be wonderful... but I've also realized and accepted that my wife makes *moi moi* [a Yoruba pudding cake] instead of *kanelbullar*."

END

Jokkmokk, Sweden

For over 400 years, the village of Jokkmokk in Swedish Lapland has held an indigenous Sámi traditional market every winter. The early February event brings in thousands of visitors, as well as Sámi from throughout the country, plus Norway, Finland, and the Kola Peninsula of Russia. Together they enjoy activities such as dogsledding, reindeer racing, cooking lessons, and tracking the Northern Lights.

At the festival, I tagged along with tour guides Matti Holmgren and Stina Svensson — and their Siberian huskies — skimming across frozen Lake Stor-Skabram. The couple lives there year-round and runs tours through their company Jokkmokkguiderna. Right before our sledding safari, a blue-eyed husky turned around and our gazes locked for a few seconds.

An instant connection was made.

THE AUTHOR

Having lived on three different continents — Africa, North America, and now Europe — for extended periods of time, Lola Åkerström is drawn to the complexities and nuances of culture and how they manifest themselves within relationships.

She holds a master's degree in Information Systems from the University of Maryland, Baltimore County. Lola worked as a consultant and programmer for over a decade before following her dreams.

Today, she's an award-winning writer, speaker, and photographer represented by National Geographic Creative. She regularly contributes to high profile publications such as *AFAR*, the BBC, *The Guardian*, *Lonely Planet*, *Travel + Leisure* and *National Geographic Traveler*.

She has received photography and writing awards, including recognition from the Society of American Travel Writers and North American Travel Journalists Association, to name a few.

In addition, Lola is the editor of Slow Travel Stockholm, an online magazine dedicated to exploring Sweden's capital city in depth (slowtravelstockholm.com). She lives in Stockholm with her husband and two children.

SPECIAL THANKS

Amanda Castleman for being my amazing editor and mentor as I put the final collection of stories together for this book.

Lilit Kalachyan for beautifully designing and laying out the visuals for this book with me.

173

Made in the USA
Monee, IL
05 May 2021